High-Impact,
Low-Carbon
Gardening

High-Impact, Low-Carbon Gardening

1001 WAYS TO GARDEN SUSTAINABLY

ALICE BOWE

Timber Press
Portland · London

Frontispiece: (right) Garden Collection/Jane Sebire; (left, above and below) Alice Bowe. Opposite: Garden Collection/Neil Sutherland. Page 6: (left) Alice Bowe; (right) Garden Collection/Andrew Lawson. Page 7: Alice Bowe. Page 9: (left) Woodhouse Natural Pools; (right) Hugo Bugg Landscapes. Pages 11-12, 25-26, 45-46, 65-66, 193-94, 213-14 © iStockphoto.com

Published in 2011 by Timber Press, Inc.

The Haseltine Building
133 S.W. Second Avenue, Suite 450
Portland, Oregon 97204-3527
www.timberpress.com

2 The Quadrant
135 Salusbury Road
London NW6 6RJ
www.timberpress.co.uk

ISBN-13: 978-0-88192-998-0

Text design by Laura Shaw Design
Cover design by Alethea Morrison
Printed in China

FSC
www.fsc.org

MIX
Paper from
responsible sources
FSC® C016973

Library of Congress Cataloging-in-Publication Data

Bowe, Alice.
  High-impact, low-carbon gardening : 1001 ways to garden sustainably / Alice Bowe. — 1st ed.
      p. cm.
  Includes bibliographical references and index.
  ISBN 978-0-88192-998-0
  1. Sustainable agriculture. 2. Gardening. I. Title.
  S494.5.S86B69 2011
  635'.048—dc22   2010048812

A catalog record for this book is also available from the British Library.

CONTENTS

Preface

HOW GREEN IS YOUR GARDEN?

Gardening is already pretty green, isn't it? Glancing out the window, I see shrubs, hedges, and trees soaking up carbon dioxide and breathing out oxygen. Like many gardeners, I was happy to get on with the job of making a beautiful garden without getting ensnared in what appears to be a complex and confusing tangle of issues relating to carbon emissions, climate change, and sustainability.

But it doesn't have to be so complicated and overwhelming. In this book I lay out ways anyone can reduce the environmental impact (and often the effort) of designing, planting, and tending a garden. I'm not going to ask you to abandon everything you like about your garden. I'm not going to ban your favourite plants or prescribe a certain look for all yards—and I'm certainly not going to compromise on good garden design (although I may have a few stern words to say about leaf blowers). Instead I examine the key concepts of sustainable landscape design and introduce the questions you need to be asking so that you can make your own choices. I promise not to be preachy or overbearing.

We'll start by looking at the basic principles of sustainable landscaping and how it differs from conventional landscaping. We'll look carefully at the management of water and compost, the sustainable gardener's two most precious natural resources. Then I talk a fair bit about choosing landscape materials. They all have an environmental impact, but some are more eco-friendly than others. I'll show you how to evaluate the degree of sustainability of each option whether you are choosing for paths, walls, decks, or driveways.

The heart of any garden is the planting. I'll introduce you to plants that can cope with extremes of weather and to the bimodal plants (which can cope with both flood and drought). We will look at the planting options and pruning tricks that will help plants cope with unpredictable weather conditions, and I'll be revealing the storm-tolerant alternatives to traditional garden classics from topiary to espaliers.

We'll also look at how you can improve the green credentials of your existing space, from ideas for green roofs and natural swimming ponds to pointers on how to improve your soil, encourage biodiversity, and maintain your garden efficiently. Above all, I give you practical advice and all the information you'll need to go out and make the right choices. We'll talk about cost-effectiveness—practical means real-world affordable—and supporting local economies. In all you'll find hundreds of tips and ideas, from easy things you can do now to deeper green possibilities you can aim for later.

Don't let buzzwords like *green*, *sustainable*, and *eco-friendly* put you off. This is essentially a book about making sound garden design choices. Let me show you how careful, considered thought about plants and materials often leads to innovative design, cost savings, and better results. Anyway, that's it for the quick tour—let's get started.

1

Improving Your Garden's Ecological Credentials

Climate change, loss of biodiversity, and resource depletion are increasingly pressing concerns. It may seem that nothing you do could possibly make a difference, but there are a number of simple choices you can make that will have a significant effect on the sustainability and ecological impact of your garden and its ability to cope with unpredictable weather conditions.

In this chapter you'll get an overview of how to redesign your garden both to improve its ecological credentials and to cope with a changing climate. We'll talk about some simple changes that can make a big difference and examine the idea of whole-system thinking as the basis of a sustainable landscape. Then you'll start right in with getting your garden down on paper and entertaining some ideas for hard landscaping and plants that make wise use of resources.

Why Bother?

Why should you care about improving your garden's ecological credentials? Green spaces provide a variety of benefits, many of which we take for granted. They make us happy and relaxed, help to foster a sense of community, and, according to some researchers, even reduce crime. In addition, a healthy landscape can actively improve our environment, by cleaning our air and water, moderating the temperature, and supporting wildlife.

Here are just some of the things that green, planted spaces do:

CAPTURE CARBON EMISSIONS. Trees and plants help to reduce the amount of carbon dioxide in the atmosphere by capturing it for use in the production of leaves, roots, and other plant materials.

MODERATE THE URBAN CLIMATE. Hedges, lawns, and other forms of planting cool the air in summer and insulate our cities in winter, mitigating the urban heat island effect.

PROMOTE HEALTH AND WELL-BEING. Gardens make us happy. Research consistently shows that they promote healing, reduce aggression, and improve concentration—whether it's a green view from a window or a walk through a local park. Green spaces with trees and plantings have been shown to reduce violent crimes and burglaries.

REDUCE ENERGY CONSUMPTION. Planting insulates our properties in the winter and cools the atmosphere in the summer, saving us money on our heating and cooling bills.

With all that gardens do for us, we owe it to ourselves to make better choices—making wiser use of resources by thinking of the system as a whole. We stand to benefit all around. Because sustainable gardening depends on reducing the input of materials and energy, it translates into less work and expense for us.

How Ecological Garden Design Is Different

The main difference between conventional and ecological garden design is the wiser use of resources. Rather than taking our natural resources for granted, we need to think of them as assets. Simple changes to traditional garden design, construction, and maintenance techniques create sustainable landscapes that use less energy, water, and other resources while generating less waste and minimizing the impact on the existing landscape. By adopting greener, more sustainable practices, we can save time and money while preserving the landscape around us for future generations.

These simple changes can make a difference:

REDUCE WATER WASTE. Billions of gallons of water can be saved globally each day by planting to suit the amount of water available in your area, harvesting water, learning when to irrigate, and controlling loss of water by wind and evaporation.

PREVENT WATER POLLUTION. We can prevent contaminated stormwater runoff from ruining our streams and rivers by reducing our use of polluting chemicals and creating rain gardens, which help to clean the water as it infiltrates back into the ground.

MINIMIZE YARD WASTE. Reusing materials on-site reduces the cost of your new landscape and saves you money on waste disposal. Make your own compost, manufacture your own soil, and think about construction for easier disassembly.

An often-cited definition of sustainable development comes from the Brundtland Commission report, *Our Common Future*, published in 1987: "Development which meets the needs of the present without compromising the ability of future generations to meet their own needs."

CHOOSE SUSTAINABLE BUILDING MATERIALS. Although deciding what is sustainable can be tough and almost every landscape material you choose to use will have some adverse impact, you can quickly determine if a material is worthy of further investigation by thinking about the energy used to source, manufacture, transport, and install the material, and about how the material behaves in the garden.

STOP DIGGING. Every time we put a spade in the soil, we damage the delicate ecosystem of earthworms, beetles, and microorganisms that keep our garden healthy. Stop walking on wet soil, put away your spade, and start mulching instead.

PUT THE RIGHT PLANT IN THE RIGHT PLACE. Choose plants that are the right scale for your garden and will thrive with the natural resources available. Pick hardy plants that can survive unexpected weather conditions and group plants together to help each other prosper by deterring pests, preventing weeds, and providing shade.

PLANT A TREE. Provide for future generations by planting a tree or two. Trees give us pleasure with their blossoms, fruit, and autumn colour. They can frame a beautiful vista, screen unsightly views, and absorb noise, and they are essential to the biodiversity of our landscapes.

MAKE ROOM FOR WILDLIFE. Add plants for wildlife and let there be some untidy areas in your garden. Even the most formal gardens can include an area where plants are left standing in the winter and where dead wood is stacked to provide a habitat for insects and other animals.

GROW YOUR OWN. Even the most beautiful plants can play a vital role in the health of a garden. Take inspiration from traditional cottage gardens and add edibles to your planting scheme. You can also have fun adding flowers for cutting, and recycling the pruned stems from coppiced plants into firewood, charcoal, building materials, and plant supports.

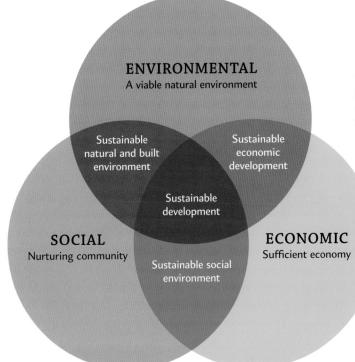

This Venn diagram is a popular way to visualize the interaction of social, environmental, and financial concerns. The area where the three circles overlap represents sustainable development. Isn't it tiny!

Basic Principles of Sustainable Landscaping

It would be so much simpler for the gardener or designer if there were a list of right or wrong ways to build and manage a sustainable landscape. If only it were that easy! With every decision, there are complex forces at play, and the best we can do is try and find our way through the maze.

A good way to consider the process of designing and enjoying a sustainable landscape is to think of it as a circle. Anything that breaks the circle should be avoided wherever possible. For example, wood is a locally grown, sustainable material that can be used to build anything from compost bins to walls to planting beds. At the end of its life it can be composted so that it can eventually nourish other plants (perhaps even trees) and enable the production of more wood for other construction projects. As soon as you paint or stain the wood, you break the circle, as you will no longer be able to compost the wood at the end of its life.

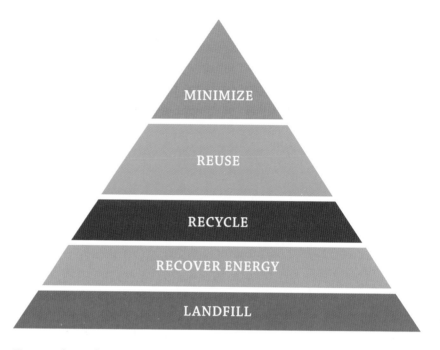

The waste hierarchy can help you make decisions about the most sustainable solution for your new garden design.

Thinking about a process as a circle is often described as whole-system thinking or systems thinking, although I prefer to think of it as futureproofing. I know it sounds a bit too much like the sort of semi-meaningless phrase you'd learn at business school, but don't dismiss it immediately—it is a very good way to understand how things influence one another in our gardens. So many of the vital processes —the water cycle, growth and decay—are cyclical rather than linear. Whole-system thinking can help us understand and work with the cyclical nature of the landscape.

Here are some basic principles to follow as you learn to think of your garden as a circle.

Use the waste hierarchy

The idea of a waste hierarchy is that the more efficient the use of resources, the more sustainable that practice is. For example, prevention consumes the least energy and produces the least waste, while disposal is the most wasteful. In addition, the most sustainable practices reduce emissions, reduce hazardous materials, and protect soils and groundwater.

When using the waste hierarchy to help you make decisions about materials, remember to think not only about your choice of material now but also about how the material might be reused at the end of its current life. Where possible, materials should be reused at the start and end of the life of the garden (back to whole-system thinking!). When considering materials you want to use, keep asking yourself if you can reuse or repurpose a material to begin with and if this material can be recycled into something useful later. Will you be able to compost it at the end of its life, or is it destined for the landfill?

Design construction for disassembly

Once you have come to grips with the waste hierarchy, you can start to include these principles in your design decisions by designing your garden for eventual disassembly. Your typical garden chair, even if constructed from wood rather than plastic, will have weatherproofing chemicals, bolts, nails, or other metalwork. All these things make it more difficult to disassemble for reuse or recycling. A more sustainable construction would be to use an unstained, durable timber fixed with wooden pegs. Larger structures, such as a pergola, might employ mortise-and-tenon joints. Fences might benefit from a rammed earth foundation rather than concrete footings around the main fence posts. Better still, consider a hedge or living willow fedge.

Think in terms of product life cycle

One way to evaluate the sustainability of a product is to look at the energy and resources used over its lifetime. This is discussed in many ways: as embodied energy, energy returned on energy invested (EROEI), and cradle to grave. The embodied energy of a building material is a calculation of the total energy consumed (and carbon released) over its life cycle. In some cases this includes all energy used from extraction of the raw materials to the end of the product's lifetime (cradle to grave), while in other cases this includes all energy consumed up to arrival at the building site (cradle to site). When using embodied energy as a measure to compare the sustainability of products, make sure you know which one they are talking about—you may not be comparing like with like.

GREEN TIP **Check the environmental credentials of building materials you are considering using. The BRE Green Guide to Specification (www. bre.co.uk/greenguide/podpage. jsp?id=2126) provides summary environmental ratings (based on life cycle assessment) of the main building materials and is a fantastic reference when you're choosing materials for your hard landscaping (or hardscape).**

Choose local materials

A lot of noise is made about the advantages of using local materials. In our global economy, thinking locally can simply be a way to think about the resources of your country rather than relying on overseas imports. Transport miles are important, but the mode of transport is just as important—for example, sea freight uses only a small fraction of the energy required to shift heavy loads on the road. And the environmental costs of local materials need to be weighed in the balance. Despite this, many gardeners still overlook the most local resources of them all—those already on-site.

Take a look around your garden. In a typical yard you might find a patch of lawn, some soil or rubble, perhaps some concrete or paving, and the odd brick. Time to order a skip, you may be thinking. Take a fresh look, and you should see a wealth of opportunity.

Treat water and waste as a resource

The waste hierarchy can also be applied very successfully to address the issues of drought and flood. If you start thinking about water as a resource, you will find it much easier to remember that the best choice is to design a garden that doesn't need any extra water. Next best is to design a garden that reduces its water requirements, perhaps by using drought-tolerant planting. One step down from this is to reuse water within the garden to supplement your need. You can do this by harvesting rainwater from your guttering and collecting it in water barrels for later use.

The same rules apply to waste. Think about all plant material as a resource. The most sustainable gardens are designed not to need any additional compost, topsoil, mulch, or fertilizers to be brought in from off-site. Next best is to design a garden with some provision for composting and reusing material on-site even if this need is supplemented by buying in local compost. Dead plant matter—be it grass clippings, old turf, prunings, fallen leaves, or just unwanted plants—can all be turned into lovely compost and used to mulch and enrich the soil. You can even compost kitchen waste with the right composting system (more on this in the next chapter). One step down from this is to buy in locally composted green waste or spent mushroom compost from a local mushroom farm.

(top left) This old bath makes an attractive garden pond. Garden Collection/Gary Rogers

(top right) These plastic bottles have been recycled into protective mini cloches in this kitchen garden—perfect for winter lettuce.

(center right) Wooden pallets can be used to make an inexpensive compost bin.

(bottom left) Wine bottles can be reused to make an attractive path edging—but are best avoided as a lawn boundary—lawnmowers and glass bottles don't mix! Garden Collection/Liz Eddison

THE SUSTAINABLE SITES INITIATIVE

While standards exist for sustainable structures—"green buildings"—there have been no comprehensive guidelines and performance benchmarks for those who want to create and measure sustainable landscapes—until recently. The U.S.-based Sustainable Sites Initiative rating system assesses specific site performance on a 250-point scale, with points awarded based on credits covering such areas as site selection, use of materials, restoration of soils and vegetation, and sustainable practices in construction and maintenance.

The central message of the Sustainable Sites Initiative is that any landscape—whether the site of a large subdivision, a shopping mall, a park, an abandoned rail yard, or even one home—holds the potential both to improve and to regenerate the natural benefits and services provided by ecosystems in their undeveloped state.

Where Do I Start?

Whether you are renovating your landscape or creating a new garden from scratch, there is no need to abandon conventional design rules. Start by assessing which parts of the garden you like and then identify any opportunities for improvement. Draw up a list of features you would like to include in your new garden and sketch a scale plan of your site on a piece of graph paper so that you can try out various options before beginning any heavy lifting.

At this point, it is also important to assess the natural resources available to the garden. How much rainfall can you reliably expect your garden to receive? Is the site flat or sloping? How exposed is the site? How many hours of sunshine does the garden get? Make a quick list of the materials you already have in the garden. This list might include stone, gravel, concrete, bricks, and wood. Write down everything. Don't forget to add any pots and planters, garden structures—even soil, plants, and turf.

Winter structure

Winter structure is the backbone of a good garden design, and it is the first thing I design into any garden scheme. Some of these structures are permanent walls and seats, while others are plant-based—hedges, arches, beds, and borders. Much of the structure of the garden will be

(top left) You don't have to rely on evergreens for winter structure—here the golden seed heads of *Stipa gigantea* are punctuated by the dark central cones of daisies whose petals have long fallen off.

(top right) Amsonia is one of the hardest-working perennials in the garden. Tolerant of sun or semi-shade, moist soil and drought, it holds dense clusters of starry flowers from spring to midsummer before the foliage flames yellow for autumn.

(bottom left) Penstemon will happily flower throughout the summer—even in drought.

(bottom right) Heuchera is a reliable foil for any planting and will stand up to almost any weather condition you can think of.

soil. You won't need to get involved with the fine detail of your planting scheme at this stage, but it is definitely worth starting to make a wish list of the plants that will thrive in your garden so that you can begin to swap plants and collect seeds and seedlings from friends.

Match your wish list of plants to the resources available on-site, choosing plants that suit the water available, the exposure and aspect, as well as the likelihood of flood, drought, or fire. Be ruthless. Only hardworking plants that suit your site deserve a place in the greener garden. Don't worry if you end up with unwanted donations from well-meaning friends and neighbours—just use whole-system thinking and remember, unwanted plants make lovely compost!

With ideas about your new garden design beginning to simmer, it's time to go right back to basics to talk about the water cycle and making compost.

Managing Essential Resources:
Water and Compost

You've already read a little about responsible use of water and how to use the waste hierarchy to make decisions in designing your garden. In this chapter we will look at water use in more detail and discuss how the same principles can be applied to disposal of garden waste. The two topics may not at first appear to be linked, but the same basic rules apply. Both processes are based on a continuous cycle, and so they are a great way to start thinking about whole systems before we move on to some of the more complex questions of sustainable landscaping materials.

Water: Managing Our Most Precious Resource

Water is the most important natural resource available to gardeners. It is literally the stuff of life. Although you can't control the amount of rain that falls on your garden, you can make the most of the water you receive.

We all learn a little about the water cycle at school. Three-fourths of the earth's surface is covered in water: it evaporates, forms clouds, falls back to the earth as rain, and then filters down through the soil and back into the water table. Ninety-nine percent of this water is not available for us to use—it's in salt water oceans, the polar ice caps, and snow up on Everest, for example—so we need to make the best possible use of the remaining 1 percent.

When it rains, water soaks into the ground or is captured by gutters and drains and sent down into the storm drains. From a gardener's point of view, any water that is sent into the drainage system is wasted. If it doesn't wet the soil, it can't help plants in the garden. The best use of resources is to use any rain that falls to irrigate our gardens and nothing else. This is easy to do by creating permeable surfaces (more on that in the next chapter) and learning how to harvest and store excess rainwater for later use.

You already have a good idea of the levels of rainfall you can expect where you live. Here in the English Midlands, it's reliably wet all through the year. If you live in the Southwest of the United States, you're used to extended periods of drought punctuated by monsoon rains. Understanding the local weather system helps you choose the plants that will thrive in your garden, but as the climate becomes less and less predictable, more and more gardeners will need to cope with both heavy rainfall and long droughts.

Watering efficiently

Water is a limited resource, and I am sure I am not alone in sometimes taking it for granted, despite trying to use water in a less wasteful way. The U.S. Environmental Protection Agency (EPA) estimates that at least half the water we use on our landscapes is wasted through overwatering and evaporation. Understanding how water works in the landscape makes a huge difference to the way we use water in our gardens.

Preparations for an efficient watering regime start at the design stage. When planning your garden, you can save water by grouping the thirstiest plants in depressions or areas that receive water from slopes or downspouts when it rains. Shelter the most water-demanding plants from moisture-sapping winds by positioning drought-tolerant plants to the north and west of them to make a miniwindbreak. If you group plants with similar moisture requirements together in hydro-zones, you will be able to target any additional watering to only the plants that

In this Chelsea show garden by Tom Stuart Smith, the zinc metal tanks that punctuate the planting double as water reservoirs.

GREEN TIP Group plants with similar moisture requirements together in hydro-zones. Group the thirstiest plants in areas that receive rainwater runoff, and position drought-tolerant plants to the north and west of more water-demanding plants to shelter them from moisture-sapping winds.

Check to see how much water is available by poking a finger deep into the soil at the base of a plant. If there is soil stuck to your finger when you pull it out, there is plenty of moisture still available in the soil.

A study by the Water Conservation Department in Austin, Texas, demonstrated that most homes were using twice as much water for landscape irrigation as the local conditions required. After the homeowners in this study were informed of this overwatering, their average water use in the garden declined by 37.5 percent in the next month.

Research by the U.S.-based Irrigation Association has shown that as much as a third of the water used to irrigate gardens is lost to evaporation in the middle of the day.

need it. The inclusion of water barrels, swales, and a drainage scheme for your rainwater runoff should augment this effectively.

Plenty is said about watering the garden, but plants actually die more often from too much water than too little. When we overwater the garden, the soil becomes saturated, forcing out oxygen. The plants then drown. You can keep an eye on the water levels in your soil by installing a simple rain gauge or by using the finger test. You will be surprised how long water reserves remain in well-structured soil—you may need to water less than you thought.

How do we choose the best way to apply water when our plants do need a drink? In hot weather, especially in the midday sun, plants can look a bit limp. It is tempting to rush out immediately and give your plants a soak. Unfortunately, when you water your garden in the middle of the day, much of the precious fluid is lost to evaporation. A far better choice is to wait until nightfall or early morning, when the ambient temperature is cooler, winds tend to be calmer, and less water is wasted to evaporation. If you are wedded to an irrigation scheme, make sure it is programmed with a rain gauge and timer so that you do not overwater.

If we look to nature, we can see that natural planting season often coincides with heavy bursts of natural rainfall. This encourages plants to send out roots in all directions, exploring the soil to find any available water. If we are to use water efficiently in the garden, we need to follow the same principles, watering deeply and infrequently to encourage roots to tap into the water table deep underground, where water levels are consistently higher.

The mistake many gardeners make is to water often and too lightly. You may be surprised to realise that you may have to water for ten minutes before the soil at the upper level is saturated. Many of us water for only a few seconds, or minutes at the most, which may do more harm than good. With light watering, the water rarely soaks far enough into the ground for a strong root system to develop, so the plant is reliant upon roots near the surface to keep it alive. Since a high proportion of the water at these upper levels is lost to evaporation, these pampered plants will need watering daily to stay in good health. This gets gardeners into the bad habit of watering too frequently, thinking that they are doing the best thing for the plants in their care.

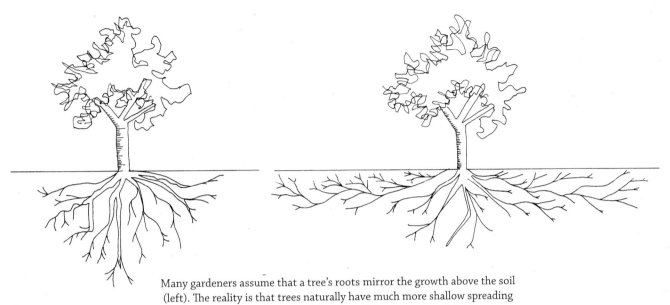

Many gardeners assume that a tree's roots mirror the growth above the soil (left). The reality is that trees naturally have much more shallow spreading root systems that extend far beyond the tree canopy (right).

A far better approach is to water deeply and less often. Water at the roots until the soil is saturated, then don't water again for a few days. The way to ensure water is reaching the deepest levels is to carry on until water begins to run off the surface. This shows that the top levels are saturated. After a period without rain, this can take as long as ten minutes. Then stop watering and allow it to soak in for thirty minutes to an hour. When you return, you will only need to water for half the time.

Deep watering will encourage deep rooting, which will lead to stronger, healthier plants—and just think of all the time you will save! You can see this best in times of drought. Pampered plants with shallow roots will begin to wilt and die after only a few days, whereas plants with a strong, deep root system will be happy for weeks or months because their roots are hooked into the water table deep underground.

Irrigation or watering can?

There is a whole industry devoted to the irrigation of domestic gardens, and nowhere is this more prevalent than in the United States. Is there

GREEN TIP Add organic matter to the soil to increase water retention so that plants will have access to it for longer.

Water deeply and infrequently to encourage deep roots. Water at the roots until the soil is saturated, then don't water again for a few days.

Instead of watering potted plants from above, try dunking them to save water and ensure they get a thorough drink. Submerge the pot in a bucket of water. When the bubbles disappear, take the plant out and do the next pot.

any place for irrigation in the greener garden, or should we be reaching for the good old-fashioned watering can?

Sprinklers, in my opinion, are never a good idea. They are expensive, they are noisy, they cause huge amounts of water to be lost by evaporation, and they can also encourage fungal infections to take hold. Water is the most common way for disease to move around the garden, and the longer a plant stays wet, the more susceptible it is to infection.

Drip irrigation or porous pipes can be a helpful way to automate the watering process as they can be set up with a timer and rain gauge so that they adjust the watering regime in relation to the rainfall and climate, and water at night when the least amount of water will be lost. The direct application of water to the roots (exactly where it is needed) means that porous pipes are pretty efficient, but the American Water Works Association still advises that yards with drip systems use 16 percent more water than those without any irrigation. Drip irrigation and porous pipe systems are quite cheap but they are often unnecessary, and on a large project small costs mount up.

The ideal is to water your garden using rainwater alone. A well-designed garden planted at the correct time of year (when natural rainfall is at its peak) should not need any additional water, aside from a good soaking on the day it is planted. If you are unlucky enough to encounter an unexpected period of dry weather, you may need to hand water for the first few months while the plants are becoming established. Fingers crossed the natural rainfall will sort you out, though; a newly planted garden can take hours to water properly if you can't rely on the weather. Occasional watering is best done with a watering can, or with a wand attachment from your water barrel, right at the base of the plant.

As the process of irrigating our gardens and landscapes has become easier and more automated, the number of landscapes across the world being overirrigated has increased significantly. Stop and think about whether you really need additional watering—less is often more!

Rainwater collection

In times of drought, we may need to provide extra water to plants in our garden. Planning ahead, by including water barrels and pools, is vital. Most of us already have a very sophisticated form of guttering on our homes, which successfully harvests water from our roofs every time it

For gardeners hoping to survive periods of low rainfall or drought, a rainwater barrel or reservoir is essential.

(top left) Rain chains are a beautiful and functional alternative to traditional closed metal or plastic downspouts. A reclaimed and painted wooden barrel is a classic choice for rainwater collection. For a stylish twist, why not paint your drainpipes to match? Garden Collection/Liz Eddison

(top center) You can commandeer almost any large container as a water reservoir. Metal vessels, like this old planter, often develop a beautiful patina. Garden Collection/Neil Sutherland

(top right) This reclaimed oil drum makes a great impromptu water barrel.

(lower left) You can fill a watering can directly from a rainwater barrel simply by turning on the spigot.

rains, but most of us don't make full use of it. Connecting a water barrel to the downpipe of a house, garage, or shed is simple. The easiest way to do it is to remove the bottom portion of your downpipe and feed the remaining portion straight into the water barrel. Alternatively, you can buy a downpipe diverter from your local hardware store. These fit onto your drainpipe, and the fanciest versions even include leaf filters and/ or an automatic overflow that sends water down the drain once your water barrel is full. The water is always ready to use, and the barrel will quickly fill up after a downpour.

There is a vast array of water tanks to choose from, whether you go for a specially designed plastic water barrel, a reclaimed distillery barrel, or a metal trough. Even in the smallest of gardens, you might find that a single water barrel isn't enough; if you need more, it is easy to slot water storage devices into your garden design and even make them a feature.

In other parts of the garden, you might choose to disconnect your downspouts so that they directly irrigate planted borders each time it rains. You could use a rain chain to channel the water into a temporary water feature, but make sure you include an overflow to extra storage or storm drains; that way your water feature can cope with a full-on cloudburst.

Reusing grey water

Rainwater is not the only water you can collect for use in the garden. Grey water (water that has already been used but can be reused—just not for drinking) can be saved from baths, washing machines, and sinks. Most shampoos and soaps will be dilute enough to cause no harm if the grey water is used in the garden. If you are planning on using the water from your washing machine, it is best to choose a detergent that is low in phosphorous and sodium. It is also best to avoid very greasy water from your washing up (although the rinsing water is perfect).

Many gardeners choose to take their grey water out into the garden in a bucket or bowl, but you can have a complete grey water system that automates the process installed in your house. Incomprehensibly, the use of grey water in the garden is illegal in many states in the United States. Contact your local authority for guidance—and lobby for new laws if necessary.

Strategies to prevent flooding

In times of heavy rainfall, one of the best ways to control the threat of flooding is to allow water to soak directly into the ground. Paving, tarmac, and concrete prevent infiltration and shed water into nearby planting beds, lawns, and drains. If much of the garden is covered in impermeable materials, problems arise when the water becomes concentrated in the permeable parts of the garden. When all the water is trying to soak into the soil in the same place, the soil quickly becomes saturated, and floods can occur. The best way to prevent flooding is to encourage the water to infiltrate over as wide a surface area as possible.

Once you have provided plenty of permeable surfaces in your garden design (50 percent is a good start), the next step is to find ways of slowing down the return of water to the ground. This may sound like a very silly suggestion indeed, but it's based on a simple premise: if we can stagger the rate at which the water hits the ground, we can help to prevent soil saturation and flooding.

The easiest way to slow down the return of water to the soil is to fill your garden with plants. Try to include a range of trees, shrubs, and perennials so that you end up with several layers of planting. When it rains, water droplets cling temporarily to leaves, branches, and stems of plants before falling to the earth or evaporating. When choosing your plants, remember to include some evergreens so that there are still plenty of plants to intercept rainfall throughout the winter months when deciduous plants have lost their leaves.

You can also slow down return of rainwater to the soil using constructed elements of the garden. Water barrels, rain chains, fountains, pools, bioswales, and rain gardens are just some of the ideas to choose from. The more layers the rain has to percolate through on its way back to the water table, the more chances we have to make use of it, and the less it will damage our landscapes in times of flood.

Bioswales and planted pockets

A bioswale is a planted depression designed to accommodate excess runoff from a house or garden. Equally important in areas with regular water shortages as it is in a wet climate, the bioswale helps us cope with unpredictable weather conditions such as flash floods. The basic idea of a bioswale is to keep rainwater on-site as long as possible so that it

GREEN TIP **Aim to make at least 50 percent of the surface of your garden permeable and then slow down the return of water to the ground by including several layers of planting and using rain chains, water barrels, bioswales, and the like.**

Swales do not hold water, so they are *not* breeding grounds for mosquitos. The water drains into the soil quickly enough that mosquitoes are not an issue.

Although a bioswale is in essence a planted ditch, it does not have to look practical and boring. Bioswales can enhance landscaping as can be seen at the Augustenborg Botanical Roof Garden and housing estate in Malmö, Sweden. Jane Sebire

has a chance to soak into the ground naturally. A successful bioswale can be as simple as a shallow drainage channel designed to carry storm water at such a gentle incline that it has plenty of time to soak into the ground before it reaches a raised drain inlet that will take any overflow to the storm drains.

Planting the swale or depression serves two main purposes: first, the vegetation slows down the flow of water (a bit like a windbreak), and second, the planting acts as a simple form of phytoremediation, cleaning the runoff water. The best planting choices for a bioswale or rain garden include plants that can cope with a degree of both drought and flood. Many of these are native wetland plants, such as iris or reeds.

(top) By recycling your waste materials on-site you will close the nutrient circle and save the cash you would have spent on compost, mulch, and topsoil.

(right) Compost improves soil structure and gives your plants access to the water and nutrients they need.

Compost: Cycling Garden Waste

Now that you have learned to manage the cycle of water in your garden, it's time to look at plant waste. In line with whole-system thinking, you want to keep garden waste on your land and use it to manufacture soil. One of the best ways to improve the ecological credentials of your garden is to start making your own compost. Don't listen to any of the horror stories—it really isn't as tricky or smelly as people would have you believe. In fact, by following some simple rules, you'll soon be a bona fide composting expert. By recycling your waste materials on-site you will close the nutrient circle, using your own materials to replenish the soil—and saving all the cash you would have spent on compost, mulch, and topsoil.

Compost is a living system; millions and millions of tiny composting creatures live, feed, and breed in your compost. Compost is great for the soil. It improves soil structure and helps to increase its water-holding capacity, giving your plants access to the water and nutrients they need.

A study by the Waste and Resources Action Programme in March 2007 found that households in the United Kingdom throw away about a third of the food they buy. About half of the 6.7 million tonnes of food thrown in the bin each year is edible and the rest comprises waste such as peelings and bones. According to a 2004 study by anthropologist Timothy Jones of the University of Arizona Bureau of Applied Research in Anthropology, U.S. households on average waste 14 percent of their food purchases, tossing meat, fruits, vegetables, and grain products in the garbage.

What to compost?

OK
- cardboard (make sure it is torn or crumpled)
- coffee grounds and teabags
- eggshells
- grass clippings
- green waste (soft leafy plants, annual weeds, fruit and vegetables)
- leaves (some OK; better composted on their own to make leaf mould)
- newspaper (although this is better sent for recycling)
- poultry manure and bedding
- wood ash (in moderation)

NOT OK
- coke and coal ash
- disposable diapers
- meat, fish, dairy (can attract vermin and smell terrible; OK for bokashi composting)
- perennial weeds
- plastics

The correct provision of compost heaps is essential to the design of every garden, large or small. There are lots of different composting methods, depending on the time you have to put in and the waste materials you are generating. Often it will be most appropriate to use several methods in combination. I am always surprised by the amount of waste material even the smallest of gardens is able to generate, so it is a good idea to always overestimate your composting requirements. There is no such thing as too much compost.

The case against burning

Burning garden waste is an age-old tradition with its roots in farming, but this polluting activity is being outlawed in more and more localities. Open burning fills the air with toxic chemicals, soot, particulates, and greenhouse gases. Compared with closed burning in an incinerator, open burning is a very inefficient process, and it often does not burn waste completely. Emissions from bonfires can have damaging health effects, and a number of papers have been published in recent years highlighting the danger of toxic emissions and fine particulates that result from open burning. The particulates cause problems for sufferers of asthma and other respiratory diseases.

Rather than burning garden waste, why not transform it into rich soil conditioner? Woody garden waste (branches, hedge clippings, and such) can be shredded or chipped and then added to your compost heap as normal or used as mulch. If you have a lot of woody waste and plenty of space, it might be worth making a compost heap just for larger pieces of wood. It will take much longer to rot down than other composting methods (it can take a few years) so you might want to hide it away in part of the garden you don't use that much. If you don't have that much space, your local waste management authority will be only too happy to compost it for you.

If you are feeling adventurous, why not try making a German mound? Dig a circular trench and make a pile of woody material in the centre. Top this mound with turf (face down), then add layers of leaves and compost before finishing off the pile with a layer of topsoil. You will be able to grow hungry, shallow-rooting crops (such as strawberries or zucchini) in your German mound as the layers slowly break down, releasing nutrients and creating lovely rich compost.

Cold compost

Cold compost is one of the easiest types of compost to make. It does not require complex layering or turning. Most gardeners choose to make their compost in a bin. This is not strictly necessary; you can just build a heap and cover it with some plastic or cardboard, but compost bins are neater and easier to manage. Cold compost heaps can vary dramatically in size but I wouldn't recommend a compost bin much smaller than 75 × 75 × 75 cm (about 2.5 × 2.5 × 2.5 ft). I like to use a linear series of wooden bins so that I can fill one bin while the second is composting. Commercially available wooden bins can rarely be found in sizes larger than 1.2 m (about 4 ft) square and deep, so if you want something larger, you may have to make it yourself. Cold compost bins do not generate heat, so they are best in a shady spot.

You can add all your garden waste and kitchen scraps to the compost heap, plus any cardboard toilet paper rolls, egg cartons, cereal boxes, and other pieces of card. Layer up the compost materials as and when you generate them, remembering to scrunch any flat cardboard into loose balls (to create air pockets that the composting creatures will love). The waste generated by an average household tends to create a pretty balanced mix of ingredients, but if you find your cold compost heap is too wet, add some more cardboard—and if it gets too dry, add some more kitchen or garden waste. It's as simple as that.

Don't add weeds or diseased material to your cold compost heap, as they will not be killed by this composting process. Add them to a hot compost heap instead, or put them in your green recycling bin for the city to take away and add to their hot compost heap.

Hot compost

If your compost gets too slimy using the cold composting method—too many grass clippings, perhaps?—you may prefer to use the hot composting method. Hot composting uses alternate layers of flat cardboard and vegetative waste to transform your waste materials into dark, friable compost. Unlike the cold composting system, which relies on trapped pockets of air and a cool temperature, hot composting traps heat between the layers to create a hot, anaerobic atmosphere that attracts a completely different set of hungry composting critters.

As with cold composting, a bin is not required but can help to keep the process looking neat and to insulate the heap so that your compost

GREEN TIP Instead of burning woody garden waste, shred or chip it before composting or bury it in a German mound.

If you decide to buy a compost bin, there are lots of designs to choose from. Some local authorities offer cheap compost bins as part of their campaign to promote recycling.

(top left) In a small garden, you might want to disguise your compost bin as a beehive. Garden Collection/Liz Eddison

(top center) Woven hazel (hazelnut) compost bins are easy to make and easy on the eyes. Garden Collection/Derek St Romaine

(top right) When collecting kitchen waste for the compost, keep it covered at all times to prevent flies. Garden Trading

(bottom) Anecdotal evidence suggests compost tea works miracles in the garden, but the evidence is still inconclusive.

heats up more quickly. Some gardeners choose to use a dark-coloured plastic bin in a sunny spot, while others choose wooden bins with an insulating lid or quilt on top. Hot compost bins can go much larger than cold compost bins—in fact, the larger the bin, the more quickly it will heat up and the more rapidly your garden waste will break down. Anaerobic fungi and bacteria break down the compost materials, and this process generates even more heat. If the fungi and bacteria get too hot, they die, so it is vital to turn the compost heap once a week to introduce some cool air.

I use a linear arrangement of 1 × 1 × 1 m (about 3 × 3 × 3 ft) compost bins for my hot compost so that I can fill one bin while the second one is composting. Each week I simply turn the contents of the second bin into the third, and the first bin into the second. Working on this scale, it is easy for me to manage the hot compost heaps by myself—and the longer your series of bins, the easier it is.

Because the hot composting method generates tremendous heat, you can be sure that weeds (roots and seeds) in the compost heap will be destroyed. Diseased plant material can also be disposed of without concern. The hot compost method requires a lot more attention than cold compost (which you can just feed and forget), but it can produce lovely, rich compost in only eight to ten weeks.

The quick return compost method

The quick return compost method was developed by Maye Bruce in the 1930s as a response to the emerging biodynamic theories of Rudolf Steiner. Key to the success of this hot compost heap is the use of the flowers and leaves of five common herbs (chamomile, dandelion, valerian, yarrow, and nettle), plus powdered oak bark, seaweed, and honey, as an herbal activator. The incredible thing about the quick return compost method is that compost can be made in a matter of weeks, without turning and without the need for manure.

Instructions for building a quick return compost pile are included on every packet of QR activator. Although Maye Bruce's original book has been out of print for many years, her quick return compost method has claimed a cult following since its invention. A revised edition of the classic, edited by Andrew Davenport and available on his QR Composting Solutions website, should raise the profile of this simple and essential composting system. Andrew Davenport has also written his

GREEN TIP Add your own weeds to your hot compost. Because weeds often accumulate the minerals that they have taken from the soil, this can be a good way to correct any soil deficiencies.

GREEN TIP **QR activator for quick return compost is available online. Get QR activator in the United Kingdom from Chase Organics (www.chaseorganics.co.uk) or QR Composting Solutions (qrcompostingsolutions.co.uk). In the United States, try Greenfeet (www.greenfeet.com) or Peddler's Wagon (www.peddlerswagon.com).**

own book on Maye Bruce and the composting method, called *Quick Return Compost Making*.

Leaf mould

Autumn leaves litter our gardens, but burning or binning these dead leaves is a false economy. Don't spend hours trying to get rid of the leaves from your yard. Instead, stuff them into bags where they will rot down to make a brilliant, free soil conditioner with very little effort.

While small quantities of leaves can be added to your compost heap to balance out wet and soggy materials such as grass cuttings, it is far better to leave a glut of leaves to rot separately and make leaf mould or "black gold." Unlike the heat-generating bacterial activity of compost heaps, rotting of leaves tends to happen by the slower and cooler reaction of fungi.

Making leaf mould can be as simple as stuffing fallen leaves into a black garbage bag, watering them well, and abandoning them in a shady corner of the garden or under a hedge for a couple of years. Better still, use a loosely woven jute bag that will biodegrade at the same speed as your leaves. Shredded leaves break down more quickly than whole leaves, so run a lawnmower over fallen leaves before collecting them to speed up the process. For larger gardens, you might find it easier to construct giant leaf mould cages from coppiced hazel or chicken wire. I like to collect my autumn leaves after a spot of rain; this speeds up the whole process since I then don't have to add any water myself.

Some gardeners choose to leave fallen leaves where they land, mimicking the tried-and-tested ecosystem of a woodland or rain forest. This allows them to take advantage of the protective, insulating qualities of the leaves and protect plant roots from frost damage. Don't be put off by claims that bad fungi and pests lurk in layers of fallen leaves—healthy leaves are an asset to the gardener. Only if your plants are already suffering from mites, blight, or the like will you need to remove fallen leaves, along with any other infected material, so that they can be composted at high temperature.

The ingredients of leaf mould are plentiful in the autumn months and very easy to get hold of. If the leaves in your garden don't satisfy your appetite for leaf mould, why not offer to sweep up your neighbour's garden in return for the leaves? Contact your local council or cemetery for spare autumn leaves. They are usually pleased to find a home for garden waste they would otherwise have to pay to send to the landfill.

Leaf mould makes an excellent soil conditioner and mulch. You can substitute it for peat and use it in seed and potting mixes. For seed sowing, use leaf mould on its own, or mixed with equal parts sharp sand and garden compost. For a potting compost, mix equal parts well-rotted leaf mould, sharp sand, loam, and garden compost.

Compost tea

The jury is still out on compost tea. Popular with organic growers, it is made by steeping ordinary compost in cold water to increase the microbial composition. Once the tea has been brewed, it is applied as a foliar spray or soil drench.

Compost teas have acquired an almost mythical reputation for the promotion of plant growth and prevention of fungal diseases such as mildew, but at present there is little independent evidence to back up these claims. Equally, we still don't know whether anaerobic compost tea can harm plants, or the benefits and dangers of additives such as molasses and kelp, as well as the potential for problems like damping off (fungal attacks that can kill seeds or seedlings). Despite many rumours, there is no evidence to support or quash concerns that use of compost tea on food plants can cause food poisoning. Research is currently being undertaken around the globe to provide scientific knowledge supported by controlled, replicated experiments to back up this wealth of practitioner-based knowledge.

The potential benefits of compost tea are thrilling enough to keep a gardener awake at night. Compost teas could be brewed specifically to match the requirements of the soil or plant; they could even be injected into paving for street trees. Current findings seem to suggest that the safety and benefits of compost tea relate directly to the quality of the compost used—and this would make sense. But while the debate rages and research continues, why not consider making a foliar drench from comfrey or borage?

Wormeries and vermicompost

Most gardeners know that worms are a great indicator of healthy soil. This is because worms consume microbes that are themselves consum-

GREEN TIP Let leaves lie where they fall or stuff them into black garbage bags to rot down over time into rich leaf mould.

GREEN TIP **Search out a wormery system that comes with tiger worms rather than the cheaper and more widely available dendrobaena worm (also known as the European night crawler) commonly used by anglers. Tiger worms, which breed exceptionally well, are hungrier and tolerate a wider temperature, moisture, and acidity range than their cousins.**

ing decaying plant matter. Worms rid themselves of their waste in the form of casts; these are enhanced with many more microbes, and this helps to speed up the decay process. Worms can also help us compost waste material such as vegetable peelings, torn pieces of cardboard, and even bones, if we can replicate their natural habitat in a wormery.

The best worms for vermicomposting systems are epigeic worms (worms that live on or near the surface of the ground), such as the tiger worm (*Eisenia fetida*). These worms are native to the United Kingdom and North America and occur naturally outdoors wherever there is organic waste, such as in your compost heap. This type of worm likes to live in the topsoil and loose organic litter on the soil surface, an environment that can easily be duplicated in a well-designed wormery bin or composting system. Tiger worms feed on the food waste and convert it into leachate (a concentrated liquid feed) and bio-rich vermicompost.

It is not a good idea to collect worms from your garden to use in your wormery unless you are an expert at identifying them. Many of the most commonly found garden worms are deep-burrowing worms that will not survive in the confines of a wormery. When you buy your wormery (online is your best bet), all reputable suppliers should provide you with an initial stock of small-to-medium-sized young (hungry) worms. A good guide is to stock a 70-litre (20-gallon) wormery (ideal for a small household) with 500 g (1000 worms).

I like stacking wormeries as I find them easier to manage than bin-type wormeries. The worms enjoy increased air flow and surface area—and the trays are easier to manage and empty. Three trays are ideal: the top one for active composting where the new waste is added, the middle one for the worms, and the bottom one for drying or draining your compost. The basic principle is that as the worms climb upward searching for organic waste, they leave worm casts behind. Liquid drips through the bottom tray, where it can be tapped off and used as a liquid drench, and the worm casts in the bottom layer dry out for use as compost. When the bottom tray becomes full of compost, you can use it in the garden and put the empty tray back on the top of the stack, ready to be filled with more kitchen waste. It's that simple.

The best place to site your wormery is somewhere handy (so that you can be bothered to use it), although some gardeners like to put it in a greenhouse or potting shed for the winter to moderate the temperature. Try to avoid full sun (especially in summer) or your worms might

The worms that are being added to this wormery will soon start to consume decomposing kitchen waste, which they will turn into lovely rich compost. Fantastic! *Garden Collection/Marie O'Hara*

overheat. If you are leaving your wormery outdoors all year, you can protect your worms from the worst frosts by insulating it with a couple of layers of old bubble wrap and jute sacks or horticultural fleece. The worms will hibernate in the very cold snaps but will soon thaw and start chomping again.

Occasionally, you may get visitors to your wormery in the form of flies or maggots. These usually result from eggs laid in the food waste that then hatch in the wormery. The best way to prevent maggots is to keep your food waste covered while you are collecting it, in a bucket with a lid or covered with a cloth. If you do find flies or maggots in your wormery, you can break the cycle by covering the top layer with soil or cardboard and not adding any new waste for two to three weeks. Another good tip is to sprinkle a mix of barley and crushed limestone over your waste once a week to keep your wormery to a neutral pH, since flies love acidic conditions.

One of the most common concerns gardeners have is that the organic waste in their wormery will start to stink, but as any wormery owner will tell you, a well-designed wormery should not smell. In fact, because the decomposing waste material is actually consumed by worms, it will only smell if there is more organic matter than the worms can eat and anaerobic composting occurs. There is a simple solution for that—add more worms!

PROJECT   Make bokashi compost

To make bokashi compost, cut up kitchen waste into small pieces and add a layer to your bokashi bin. Then sprinkle a small handful of bokashi bran over the food waste. Firm it all down using the plate provided and close the lid of the bucket. Repeat until the bin is full.

Leave the full bokashi bin to ferment for two weeks while you fill a second bin. During this time, draw off any liquid that has accumulated in the bottom of the bin using the built-in tap. This makes an excellent foliar feed (diluted 1:1000) or soil drench (diluted 1:100).

After two weeks, the contents of the bokashi bin will be ready to use in the garden. You will be able to tell this by the sweet-and-sour pickled smell. You can either add it to a covered compost heap or wormery or dig it directly into trenches in the garden.

GREEN TIP Dilute your bokashi liquid feed 1:100 before using as a soil drench or liquid fertilizer or 1:1000 for a foliar feed. Undiluted, the bokashi liquid is excellent for clearing drains and blocked pipes around the home.

Bokashi

Bokashi is an increasingly popular method of intensive composting that originated in Japan, but the necessary bin and bokashi bran are now available in all good garden stores (or failing that, online at amazon). The bokashi process relies upon effective microorganisms (EMs)—including yeast, phototropic bacteria, and lactic acid bacteria, which accelerate the breakdown of food waste and effectively ferment organic matter—in the bokashi bran. You can add all your kitchen waste to a bokashi compost bin, even cooked meat and dairy, but you must not add bones or cardboard—save these for the wormery.

Bokashi is so simple and compact that it is appropriate for even the smallest of homes and gardens. The bokashi bins themselves tend to be less than 50 cm (about 1.5 ft) high. Since bokashi is a fermentation process and not true composting, there are no dodgy smells to contend with. Even my flat-dwelling sister has taken up the challenge (she says her houseplants love the diluted bokashi liquid feed, and their communal garden is benefiting from the compost).

Most people choose to use two bokashi bins in sequence, so that one is composting while the other bin is being filled. The fermenting process is very quick and your fresh bokashi compost will be ready in only a couple of weeks. Because the food waste is effectively pickled rather than composted, it will still look quite chunky at this stage, but it will break down into rich crumbly compost once it has been buried for a further month or so. I tend to add my bokashi compost to a compost bin or wormery, although you can dig it directly into the garden soil.

3

Picking Materials for Paths and Paving

With water and waste cycles understood, we now begin consideration of the materials you will use for hard landscaping (otherwise known as hardscaping) in your sustainable garden design. The materials that will form the backbone of your garden may include bricks, gravel, stone, and wood. All natural materials, you might say, but if you look a bit harder it's not quite that simple. Ask yourself three questions: How much energy was used to source and manufacture the material, and how much energy will be required to install it? How much energy was used to transport it? How will it function in my garden?

Answering these questions demonstrates just how tricky it is to make the best decisions for a greener garden. It is hard to know whether it is better to use imported sandstone with its high transport miles but the relatively low energy needed for production, or locally produced paving made from energy-intensive cement and recycled aggregate. Industry and governments are increasingly looking at product life cycles and trying to reach the answers to these questions by understanding the total impact of the product "from cradle to grave"—over its whole lifetime from production to disposal. We hope that in the future, the answer will be easier to obtain. For now, local recycled materials are the best option, where available.

Even before you choose materials for paths and paving, you ought to ask yourself how much of your garden you really want to pave. We'll start with that question here.

Less Paving, More Percolation

As garden owners aspire to increasingly low-maintenance gardens, and cheap stone imports flood the market, there has been a tendency to increase paved areas at the expense of planting. Impermeable surfaces, previously only affordable for small areas of the garden, have become commonplace as gardens are laid to paving. Even front gardens are paved over or laid with asphalt to provide additional parking.

Overpaving our landscape is an unthinking, outdated, and harmful habit. In the summer floods of 2007 in the United Kingdom, surface-water runoff was cited as the main cause of flooding in two-thirds of the 55,000 homes affected. As a result, the U.K. government has introduced new rules that make it harder to pave over front gardens without going through the planning process. Instead, we are encouraged to create gardens where the water is allowed to soak back into the soil at the source.

The rules are more variable in the United States. Some localities don't have any planning requirements—and those that do seem more focused on community aesthetics than flood defence. The City of Garden Grove in California prohibits parking on unpaved areas and stipulates that "any paving in the front yard shall cover no more than 50 percent of the yard" but makes no mention of permeability or water infiltration. Check with your own local authority for the rules that apply in your landscape; policy is moving fast in this area and it's only a matter of time before flood defences are taken more seriously.

One of the main reasons people introduce impermeable surfaces to their gardens is to provide driveways or parking spaces for cars. There are many alternatives to the traditional concrete driveway or parking area now available, including porous paving, permeable paving, grass paving, and dispersed parking. All of these strategies follow these key principles, and you should too, no matter what your paving plan:

* Manage water at the source—allow it to infiltrate where it hits the ground.

* Manage water at the surface—avoid the expense of installing and repairing pipes by moving water overland where necessary.

* Make extra water a virtue by using it to irrigate your planting areas.

Porous paving

Porous paving reduces runoff by allowing water to infiltrate through the surface of the paving. The success of this material relies on a free-draining sub-base and on the soil and natural bedrock underneath.

Porous asphalt was originally developed for airport runways, so it's pretty strong. A bed of large angular aggregate (surrounded by filter fabric to prevent sandy particles and sediment from filling the gaps) supports the asphalt and holds water while it percolates into the soil. Porous concrete works on a similar principle, but specialist advice is recommended for either of these approaches as the system can clog if not designed correctly.

GREEN TIP When designing your garden, try to at least balance the scale of permeable and impermeable areas (50 percent permeable is a good start) to give water the chance to drain away naturally

In London, 12 square miles of front garden are now paved, the equivalent of concreting over twenty-two Hyde Parks.

Permeable paving allows water to infiltrate back into the ground at source.

(top left) These slabs of reclaimed paving have been surrounded with chamomile rather than mortar to create permeable joints. Garden Collection/Nicola Stocken Tomkins

(top center) Gaps between paving slabs are filled with *Soleirolia soleirolii* (also known as baby's tears and mother of thousands, among other names), and pebbles allowing water to drain readily. Garden Collection/Liz Eddison

(bottom left) Is permeable lawn using a concrete structure better or worse than an impermeable surface using a more sustainable material? Grasscrete/Grass Concrete Limited

(top right) This small urban front garden cleverly uses wooden tyre tracks within a planted gravel garden to solve the problem of providing functional car parking facilities, permeable surfaces, and attractive planting. Garden Collection/Liz Eddison

Brick paths with sand joints allow water to infiltrate through the gaps.

Permeable paving

Permeable paving enables water to pass through the joints in the paving, although the individual components are not actually permeable. Permeable paving must be laid on a base of free-draining crushed stone or sand to allow the water that soaks through the joints to percolate into the water table. For the best results, combine small units (such as setts or pavers) with wide permeable joints.

Use a permeable joint filler, such as sharp sand, and leave the joints slightly below the level of the paving to improve the drainage. Although the joints will get filled with debris over time, and the rate of infiltration is likely to slow after five years, they will remain surprisingly permeable.

GREEN TIP **If you're building a permeable paving system, allow a 0.6-cm (¼-in) joint between pavers. Anything wider might compromise stability, and anything narrower cuts down on permeability.**

One of the phrases you will come across time and time again as you explore permeable paving is sustainable drainage systems (SUDS). These systems aim to mimic the natural movement of water through the soil back to the water table—protecting the built environment from flooding and pollution.

FRONT GARDEN DESIGN

In this show garden, metal tyre tracks allow plants to grow underneath the parking area. Heidi Harvey and Fern Alder

Modern demands for our front gardens often conflict: the need to provide off-road parking, a soothing pedestrian approach to the front door, storage for bins and bikes, planting, and a habitat for wildlife. It can be hard to work out how to balance the practical demands with aesthetics and the environment. All designers love a challenge, and some brilliant front garden solutions have been popping up as show gardens in recent years.

One elegant solution, designed by Heidi Harvey and Fern Alder for Hampton Court Flower Show in 2007, uses crushed permeable concrete and metal grills to accommodate parking and support a large area of wildlife-friendly plants. The innovation in this garden is the use of metal grids as tyre treads, which are then underplanted with a range of sedum, ferns, and succulents. Since some of the planting is sunken below the grid, it does not get damaged by vehicular traffic, but the planting does get enough light to thrive as these parking spaces are usually only used overnight and on weekends. This garden uses a variety of surfaces to break up the space and make it feel larger, but if your garden is very small you will find that a single coloured surface will make the garden feel more streamlined.

In many cases, the key is to screen the parking from the pedestrian access and prevent views of the car from inside the house. A simple way to define a path to the front door is to plant an even number of half standard trees on either side of the path, underplanted with low-growing evergreens. This design trick will lead the eye (and the visitors) to the front door.

Grass paving

Grass paving is ideal for temporary access or overflow parking. In a recent scheme for a garden I designed in the British countryside, for example, a reinforced grass track was installed to provide occasional access to the septic tank without spoiling the borrowed scenery for the rest of the year. Honeycomb cells of plastic or concrete provide enough strength to support vehicular traffic, while the permeable aggregate or planting infill allows water to percolate into the soil.

Unfortunately, I can think of plenty of examples where grass paving has been used badly. When it is used in areas of high traffic, the planting infill often gets eroded away and begins to reveal the less-than-beautiful structure beneath, as well as plenty of mud. Don't let this put you off, though—used correctly in a landscape or garden design, these honeycomb structures are a truly elegant solution for occasional vehicular routes or overflow parking. And a permeable lawn—even one constructed with a concrete structure—is always going to be a more sustainable proposition than an impermeable surface like a reclaimed stone terrace.

The most popular systems are made from precast concrete or plastic units. The thinner plastic units are most successful from an aesthetic point of view, as the large planting pockets support healthy growth that knits together to hide the plastic grid. These systems can cost up to four times as much as standard asphalt to install, but they are less costly to maintain and don't require any additional spending on drainage. Grass paving is usually best limited to light traffic, perhaps one or two days a week, as this gives the turf a chance to recover and regrow. For more frequent use, fill with an aggregate instead.

A GRASSCRETE DRIVE FOR OCCASIONAL ACCESS

In a country house in Lincolnshire, reinforced grass paving was used to link the main formal driveway with outbuildings at the rear of the property. On a day-to-day basis, the main driveway was used for guests arriving at the front of the property, and a second goods access was used for deliveries arriving at the rear of the property. The reinforced grass driveway linked these two driveways through an orchard but was used only on the rare occasions when cars needed to be stored in the outbuildings, to save them driving all the way out of the estate and all the way back in again via the alternative route.

Dispersed parking

We have already seen how the increasing demand for parking spaces poses a challenge for designers keen to prevent flooding. On a domestic scale, where only a limited number of parking spaces are required, this

GREEN TIP **Consider planting trees within any paved areas to provide pockets of permeable ground (or minibioswales) for the water to infiltrate into the ground.**

is solved by using permeable hard landscaping materials and providing ground-level planting that can absorb any additional runoff. Garden designers working on a larger scale, be it for office parking, stadiums, even public parks and historical gardens, will find the potential for flooding escalates. Dispersed parking—designing parking spaces over a larger area with planted pockets—helps to prevent flooding and can also help to protect mature trees and established planting by integrating them into the design of the new parking area.

Planted swales work particularly well in car parks, where they can help to clean rainwater runoff of the pollutants that often drip from cars. Conventional designs for car parks tend to use raised planted areas (the opposite of bioswales), forcing rainwater to run off pavement and into storm drains. If the levels were simply reversed, we could enjoy the same scale of planting in our car parks while allowing excess water to be returned to the water table.

Whether you decide to include a bioswale in your design or not, it is always a good idea to break up areas of impervious paving with porous areas that drain into the water table. It is especially important that the first flush of rain is directed to a grassy or vegetated area; the first bit of water carries away the highest proportion of pollutants, so this way most of the pollutants are kept out of the drainage system (even if some water has to overflow into the system).

Cement and Concrete

Once you've decided how much of your garden to cover with paths or paving and are down to choosing materials, one of the first stalling points you will come across is the need for cement. Cement is regularly used for the foundations of steps or the bedding of paving. It might be required for filling the joints between stone or binding the aggregate in some stone replica pavers. Cement production is a major contributor to climate change, so reducing the use of cement is one of the most important steps you can take when planning, designing, and building a more sustainable garden.

That said, there is a lot of confusion around cement and concrete: it can be hard to get your head around the difference between the two materials, which is which, which is good, which is bad, and why. In fact, it's quite simple: cement is a dry powder made from limestone. This

Cement should not be confused with concrete. Cement is a dry powder substance made from the raw material limestone in cement kilns. Concrete is a building material made from mixing cement with water and/or other filler materials such as aggregates.

powder is one of the main ingredients in a typical concrete mix but it can also be used to make mortar.

Cement is really tricky to avoid when constructing a garden because it is one of the major components used to make concrete. It is difficult to avoid using concrete because concrete is very good at its job: it is cheap and strong and durable (it can last for centuries, with limited costs for maintenance or repair), it is fire resistant, it is easy to use, and it has a high thermal capacity that enables it to absorb, store, and radiate heat. An exposed concrete shell on a building can, in many cases, eliminate the need for air conditioning and reduce heating bills. However, concrete is also very damaging to the environment because of the large amounts of CO_2 that are released during cement production, and the fact that it is hard to recycle.

During cement production, 60 percent of emissions come from the decarbonization of limestone in the kiln, meaning that "sustainable cement" can be seen as a contradiction in terms. Although producers have made progress in reducing direct emissions of carbon dioxide by investment in energy-efficient technologies, the use of alternative fuel, and the incorporation of alternative materials such as slag and fly ash, this does not change the fact that the key chemical reaction in cement manufacture emits CO_2 as a by-product.

On the positive side, cement is a locally produced material, because the key component in cement manufacture, limestone, is a commonly found raw material.

Lime as an alternative for cement

Although cement is often the default choice, you can avoid the use of cement altogether by specifying a cement alternative for mortar. Traditional lime mortar is an excellent alternative to cement and is commonly specified for historic buildings and conservation projects. Although not without environmental cost (it needs high temperatures for processing, too) it uses less energy than cement production, reabsorbs carbon, and allows for materials to be recycled at the end of their life—so it's a wonder that it fell out of favour!

Lime can be produced locally on a small scale, limiting pollution from transport and creating local employment opportunities. Strong but flexible, lime mortar prevents masonry from cracking because it is able to move with the building. Construction is also simpler with lime

GREEN TIP Reduce your use of cement in the garden by specifying lime for mortar, using cement substitutes in concrete mixes, and reusing broken-up waste concrete for paths, walls, and patios.

According to the International Energy Agency (IEA), cement production is responsible for approximately 5 percent of the world's total manmade CO_2 emissions and 2 percent of the CO_2 produced in the United Kingdom.

mortar, since it avoids the need for fiddly expansion joints and absorbs moisture, helping to keep masonry dry. Lime mortar reabsorbs carbon over its lifetime, thereby offsetting most of the initial pollution and becoming carbon-neutral.

One of the most exciting things about using lime mortar is that it allows for disassembly at the end of its life. Not only can the materials bonded with lime be reused in other structures, but the lime mortar itself can be recycled. Cement, on the other hand, sets so hard that cement-bonded equivalents can only be used as hardcore (material broken in pieces and used as a base layer).

How to make concrete more eco-friendly

Concrete is made from mixing cement with filler materials such as aggregates and water. One way to reduce the amount of cement we use is to specify cement substitutes in our concrete mixes. The most popular cement substitutes available are waste materials that would otherwise be destined for the landfill, so specifying cement substitutes promotes recycling as well as cutting down on the damaging emissions from cement production.

* Pulverized fuel ash (PFA) or fly ash is a by-product of burning coal in power stations. It is available in two classes: Type C and Type F, depending on the lime (calcium) content. Both types of PFA are routinely used to replace cement at rates of 10 to 30 percent.

* Ground granulated blast furnace slag (GGBS) is a by-product of the iron industry that can be used as a substitute for some of the cement required to make concrete. Although GGBS can replace up to 90 percent of cement, it is common practice for ready-mixed concrete companies to produce concrete with 50 percent GGBS and 50 percent cement.

* Silica fume is a by-product of the production of silicon metal and ferrosilicon alloys. Concrete containing silica fume can have very high strength and can be very durable; and if has a low water content, it is highly resistant to penetration by chloride ions.

Another way to reduce the impact of concrete in your garden is to improve the eco credentials of the other ingredients in your concrete mix. An obvious step would be to start using recycled aggregates in your mix. Aggregates—such as sand, gravel, and crushed rock—account for approximately 80 percent of a typical concrete mix, and these are all materials you might find on-site when creating a new garden. Instead of grumbling and paying to remove these materials, why not reuse them?

In the same way, concrete from demolished outbuildings, an unwanted terrace, or a crumbling garden wall can be crushed and recycled as aggregate for new construction. This still uses a lot of energy but can reduce the burden on gravel mining. In the United States, waste concrete has been given the rather more glamourous name urbanite, and it is often used to create paths, raised beds, and paving. It makes sense to reuse materials where you can, although obviously if you start transporting heavy materials such as urbanite any distance you will severely compromise your green credentials because of the fuel and transport miles involved.

Natural Stone

Now that we've dealt with the elephant in the room, we can move on to a more elegant but no less controversial material: natural stone. Natural stone paving is an obvious choice for landscape design. Although it is not cheap, it is a beautiful, classic, and rugged material—and if sourced locally it can be a very sustainable choice because it requires few or no manufacturing processes.

Most natural stone is riven (split along its natural planes), so each slab can offer huge variations in thickness. This makes it expensive to install because you will need to allow extra time to set each slab level when laying a path or terrace. You can save money on the labour costs by choosing sawn stone. This is quicker and easier to lay because it comes in a uniform size and thickness, but it is more expensive to produce.

Reclaimed stone, particularly reclaimed York paving, is highly desirable and more sustainable than newly quarried stone. However, as newly quarried York stone becomes increasingly scarce, it holds its value well and so is unlikely to be the cheapest option. If you can't get hold of locally reclaimed stone paving for your garden, locally quarried stone may be a good alternative.

Nonhydraulic lime (which needs air to set) is carbon neutral—it absorbs nearly its own weight in CO_2 in the curing process. Hydraulic lime (which doesn't require air to set and thus can be used underwater) is less efficient but can still absorb up to 75 percent of its own weight in CO_2.

Roman engineers used to make a type of concrete by combining hydrated nonhydraulic lime with a pozzolan, a finely divided material such as pumice or ground pottery that reacts chemically with the lime at ordinary temperatures and in the presence of moisture to form a strong, slow-hardening concrete. Buildings like the Pantheon in Rome were built in this way and are still standing today.

GREEN TIP Ask questions to be sure you are using locally sourced stone. Confusingly, the name bluestone can be used to refer to both a sandstone from New England and a limestone from the Shenandoah Valley, Virginia, so check what you are getting.

Whichever stone you choose to use, always remember to use the minimum thickness of stone for the job, and break up large stretches of paving with planting pockets.

Sandstone

Sandstones are particularly well suited as outdoor paving due to their good slip resistance. They are also a common choice for dressed stone (stone that is cut into blocks although the front is still rough) and dry-stone walls. York stone, Bath stone, and Portland stone are all U.K. sandstones named after their place of origin. In other parts of the world, sandstone names usually include a description of the colour, too. For instance, bluestone is probably the most popular choice for paving in New England. One of the most durable natural stones in the United States, this local sandstone is resistant to bitterly cold climates, including regular freezing and thawing.

Another popular landscaping material in the United States is local fieldstone, so called because it is usually collected from the surfaces of fields. Fieldstones are large, irregular pieces of stone that are useful in building construction. Most fieldstones have been picked up and then abandoned by glacial deposits, so they are usually roughly rectangular or rounded in shape. Fieldstones can be sandstone or quartzite—almost any type of stone, really.

Limestone

Limestone is another popular choice for paving and cladding. It can vary dramatically in colour and pattern, but pale, almost marblelike stones are some of the most popular. Limestone is a common type of stone, so you are likely to be able to find a local limestone wherever you are in the world. A word of warning, though—limestone is chemically reactive and should be avoided in areas of high pollution.

Slate

Slate is a very versatile garden material. It can either be sawn into slabs or split into thin sheets along its bedding planes. This makes it light to transport (reducing the fuel burden for deliveries) and quicker to install (reducing labour costs). Slate comes in a wide variety of colours from dark to light grey and from green-grey to plum, and is most abundant in Wales and Cumbria in the United Kingdom, China, Brazil, and across Europe. Slate is highly resistant to weathering but can become slippery when wet. It is often used in water features because it is impermeable to water.

Few slate quarries remain in the United States, but most of those that are still operating exist in the slate belt stretching across Georgia, South Carolina, North Carolina, and Virginia. Thus, local slate may not be an option for all gardens in the United States. In the United Kingdom, slate is quarried in Wales, Cumbria, and Cornwall so is much more accessible and is a popular choice with gardeners.

Granite
Granite is a very durable stone that is most commonly used as sets or cobbles. It can also be sawn or split for use as slabs or walling. Granite is very strong and keeps its sharp edges over time, so it is useful for precise and detailed work or for water features.

Colours of local granite can vary dramatically according to location. Missouri granite is usually a rich red, North Carolina is famous for its white granite, and Georgia offers grey, buff, and beige. In the United Kingdom, it's a similar tale: Lanarkshire granite is red, whereas Cornish granite is pale grey or white.

Porphyry
Porphyry is a volcanic rock that is growing in popularity among gardeners. Harder than granite, it is highly resistant to weathering and is extremely nonslip. Porphyry is known for its striking red and purple colours, but the stone can also be found in tones of green, grey, gold, brown, and black. Unfortunately for European or American gardeners, porphyry is found only in East Africa, the Antarctic, and Norway, so it is unlikely to be local to your area.

Imported stone
All across the globe, cheaper stone imports, such as Indian sandstone, are flooding the market. They appear to be a very cost-effective material to use in the landscape, but they come with a high transport and pollution impact. Besides India, China, Turkey, Brazil, and other newly industrialized countries are also expanding their natural stone production.

If you do buy imported stone, check that the importers follow an ethical code of practice such as the Ethical Trading Initiative (ETI) Base Code. Check that they also visit the country of origin regularly—

According to *From Quarry to Graveyard: Corporate Social Responsibility in the Natural Stone Sector* (2006), "Child labour is common in India's stone quarries. Children tend to start working in quarries long before they reach the age of 14 and are often made to perform hazardous tasks." If you buy setts (quarried stones) on the open market, you can be 99 percent certain they have been quarried by children.

The Indian NGO Mine Labour Protection Campaign (MLPC) has found that more than 90 percent of the mine workers in Indian stone quarries are indebted to their employers and forced to work to pay off their debts instead of receiving a wage.

both stone merchants and quarries—to check for child labour and safe working conditions. Ensure that they have their total supply chain regularly audited, work with verified nongovernmental organisations (NGOs) on community projects, and take specific steps to care for the environment.

Technical specification of stone

When buying any kind of stone, it is always important to check the technical data sheet. This will give you information on durability and performance such as slip resistance, water absorption, and porosity. You should aim to choose a stone with less than 4 percent porosity if you are planning to use it in landscaping, as stone with a higher porosity may hold water, freeze, and crack or support lichens and become very slippery and hazardous. If you are choosing to use reclaimed stone, you may find it harder to obtain this information unless you know which quarry the stone was originally from.

If you are tempted to buy cheaper imported stone, you may find that the quarry has chosen not to complete these technical data tests, as a cost-saving measure. Be aware of the gamble you are taking if you buy stone without understanding the technical specifications. What seems to be a good offer at the time of purchase may not suit your needs over the long term.

Reconstituted stone

A large percentage of modern paving in the United States and Europe is made from reconstituted stone, essentially a high-quality concrete. Reconstituted stone varies dramatically in both quality and price, and subsequently in how appropriate it is as a substitute for natural stone. At the upper end of the market, reconstituted stone can reach prices comparable to natural stone, so it will not always represent a monetary saving and it may have a greater environmental impact. If you do choose to specify a reconstituted stone for your garden, you can alleviate some of the damage by ensuring the aggregate used to make these replica pavers is reclaimed or recycled.

Fired Brick

Brick is a traditional material chosen for durability and strength. Bricks also have the benefit of absorbing heat (thermal mass) and sound (acoustic mass). Fired bricks are made from a mixture of clay and water and can be made locally around the globe. Bricks have been used in construction for thousands of years and are a popular choice for garden design where the budget allows. Each unit has been designed to be small enough so that one person can work all day without tiring but large enough to make efficient progress.

However, new bricks are not always the most sustainable choice. Brick kilns require huge amounts of energy, and if the bricks are not locally produced, more energy will be needed to transport them to their destination. In addition, bricks may need mortar to glue them together, although lime mortar can be used here to avoid cement.

When laying a brick path or terrace, you can usually avoid using any mortar at all by employing permeable sand joints instead. Designers often choose sand joints over mortar based on pure aesthetics, as violas, mosses, and other creeping plants can be encouraged to colonize the gaps, giving a garden an instant sense of history. If you want to keep your paving pristine, don't worry—if the bricks are installed on a base of sharp sand 2.5 cm (1 in) deep, weeds will not grow from the base. Some seeds may blow into gaps, but these will be shallow rooting and easy to remove if you prefer a more streamlined look.

Reclaimed bricks are a more sustainable choice than new bricks when they are sourced locally. They are durable, use little energy, and divert waste from the landfill. Where mortar is used, always specify a lime mortar, as this will allow the bricks to be reused again in the future.

GREEN TIP Use sand joints instead of mortar when laying a brick path, both to increase permeability and avoid concrete. See if you can find locally sourced reclaimed bricks instead of buying them new.

The range of aggregates to choose from is increasing.

(top left) Slate aggregate is a by-product that can also be used to make paths and planting areas.

(top right) In this small garden, slate chippings provide an important textural contrast to the slabs of slate used for the seating and paving. Generous borders balance the hard and soft landscaping. Decorative Aggregates

(bottom photos) Local stone gravel is a traditional choice (left) Garden Collection/Andrew Lawson; it is also equally at home in a contemporary design scheme (right). Garden Collection/Liz Eddison

Aggregates and Gravel

For larger areas of hard landscaping and driveways, gravel or some other aggregate may be one of the more sustainable solutions. These are permeable materials and are relatively inexpensive to install and maintain.

Primary aggregates are natural materials that have been extracted directly from quarries and marine environments, generally for use in construction. Secondary aggregates are a more sustainable choice; they include waste material from other quarrying activities, such as china clay sand and slate aggregates, as well as by-products such as blast furnace slag from the iron and steel industries. There are also recycled aggregates to consider. These vary from rubber to glass to granulated CDs—even seashells.

When specifying an aggregate for your garden design, angular materials are a good choice as they will lock together under pressure, in contrast to a rounded aggregate. Local is always preferable, but ask yourself if it would be more sustainable to use a natural stone or a recycled material.

Self-binding gravel

Self-binding gravel, which is made up of crushed stone from 1 cm (0.39 in) to dust, is an excellent choice for paving. Self-binding gravel can look excessively powdery when first applied, but as it rains (over the course of weeks and months) the smaller particles find their way down into the surface and lock the larger particles in place. After a few months, self-binding gravel forms a firm compacted surface and will stay in place without the use of cement.

On clay soils, gravel surfaces have the potential to become highly compacted and impervious under traffic, but you can reduce the risk of compaction by installing a free-draining sub-base or honeycomb support when you are building your garden.

Seashell aggregate

A natural by-product of the shellfish industry, crushed seashells make an inspired alternative to stone aggregates. Cockle shells are ideal for garden paths and driveways, locking together to form a well-drained, firm surface. Locally available seashell aggregate is a sustainable choice because it is an industry waste material that would otherwise be sent to

GREEN TIP **Give your chosen aggregate a simple rake-through once a year to help restore porosity to compacted layers.**

Some gardeners suggest that these plant losses are due to the plants' roots overheating, as the black rubber heats up unevenly, but the jury is still out on this. It is true that rubber chippings appear to prohibit the growth of moulds and fungi, but they also tend to have a very strong smell, especially in hot weather.

RUBBER MULCH AT FORT DUNLOP

At Fort Dunlop in Birmingham, United Kingdom, rubber chippings have been used to pave a courtyard of mature trees outside a Travelodge hotel. From a design perspective, the trees provide a much-needed contrast of texture and scale to the surrounding industrial buildings. The rubber mulch around the base of the (very healthy looking) trees creates a neat and low-maintenance look, while still allowing water to drain into the subsoil.

4

Covering Ground with Decks and Lawns

Continuing on the theme of thinking about the floor of your garden, we turn in this chapter to considering the use of decks and lawns to cover ground. Both can be attractive, and depending on the choices you make, both can use resources efficiently.

Decks don't have to be made of wood that robs the forests or introduces toxins to the yard; they can be made of wood that is sustainably harvested and left untreated, or alternatively treated with a nontoxic preservative or paint. Lawns don't have to be time and water sinks that are fertilized with chemicals and mowed with noisy, pollution-spewing equipment. They can be diverse, hardy plantings that do all the jobs we need a lawn to do without costing the earth. The furniture you use on decks and lawns can be sustainable as well.

Sustainable Decks

In garden construction, wood is one of the most useful materials available—and if chosen wisely, it can also be one of the most sustainable. Timber is essentially a renewable resource that can be grown and harvested locally and sustainably. Timber is an affordable material and can be used to build anything from surfaces to retaining walls, fences, furniture, structures, and even garden buildings.

That said, over the last few decades the global timber industry has been facing real problems from deforestation and the illegal logging of timber. By now, most people are aware that clearing the rain forest is a real environmental and social concern, but few realize that our insatiable demand for cheap teak garden furniture and hardwood decking is one of the main forces behind these unsustainable imports. For thousands of years forests have been soaking up CO_2, keeping the atmosphere in balance. Logging transforms trees into a source of CO_2 as decaying vegetation. The burning of trees (for example, to clear forest for ranch or grazing land) releases sequestered CO_2 back into the atmosphere. Deforestation is currently the second biggest cause of atmospheric CO_2 emissions (after power generation), and according to the Intergovernmental Panel on Climate Change (IPCC), tropical deforestation produces 20 percent of annual worldwide CO_2 emissions.

Sustainably sourced wood

Timber certification schemes are the best way to check the sustainability of any wood you are planning to buy, whether for the garden or another project. Perhaps the best known of these is run by the Forest Stewardship Council (FSC), an independent, nongovernmental, not-for-profit organization established in 1993 to promote the responsible management of the world's forests. Another important label to look out for is Programme for the Endorsement of Forest Certification (PEFC), the world's largest forest certification organisation.

Unfortunately, due to the complexity of timber supply chains, even well-respected certification schemes get it wrong some of the time. That's why furniture made from illegal timber was being sold under "sustainable" certification in Britain, according to a 2008 report from the Environmental Investigation Agency, a conservation group based in London and Washington DC. A good resource you can use to check on the true sustainability of FSC-branded products is FSC Watch, an independent observer of the Forest Stewardship Council with an excellent website that highlights potential problems with suppliers.

The best way to know exactly where your timber originated is to choose locally grown timber from a managed forest. The fewer links there are in the supply chain, the more reliable certification information will be, and if the wood is really local you will be able to see just how sustainable the forestry practices are for yourself (and you won't need to worry about road or air miles either). Among local woods, western red cedar is ideal for outdoor use. The wood contains a natural oil that acts as a preservative, and the wood itself (although a softwood) resists cracking and warping. Other popular rot-resistant softwoods include cypress, larch, Alaskan yellow cedar, Atlantic white cedar, redwood, and juniper.

Wood preservatives

Once you have struggled through choosing your wood, you reach another controversial decision, regarding wood preservatives and paints. You can avoid preservatives altogether by choosing timbers that can be used untreated outdoors such as oak, black locust, osage orange,

GREEN TIP Consult the U.S. Green Building Council's LEED (Leadership in Energy and Environmental Design) rating system for measurable criteria by which you can evaluate built elements of your landscape for sustainability.

A 2008 report by the Environmental Investigation Agency revealed that unsustainable logging is being driven by demand for wooden goods in Europe and the United States. It names the United Kingdom as the third largest importer of Vietnamese garden furniture—much of which comes from illegally logged forests in southeast Asia.

According to the U.S. International Trade Commission, as much as 30 percent of U.S. hardwood imports are from suspicious or illegal sources. The World Wildlife Fund estimates that up to 19 percent of all wood products imported to the European Union have been sourced illegally.

GREEN TIP **Whenever possible, choose locally grown timber from a managed forest. Urban timber (timber made from trees cut down for various reasons in urban areas) is another good product available in a few areas.**

Check that your timber is FSC or PEFC certified. You should find the labels stamped on the wood or the packaging.

sweet chestnut, western red cedar, larch, and Douglas fir. These look beautiful in a garden and age to a beautiful silvery grey.

If you do choose to treat your timber, it is best to avoid all commercial timber preservatives. These are chemical fungicides and pesticides that may leach out and contaminate the soil or water table. As soon as you treat timber with chemicals, you are ensuring it is destined for the landfill. Chemical treatment of timber prevents you from recycling the wood as compost, mulch, or fuel at the end of its life, so it's not very sustainable. Try raw linseed oil instead. If you must use preservatives, use one of the boron-based compounds. Boron compounds are well-known nontoxic preservatives that are often combined with linseed oil and plant resins to make eco-friendly preservatives—but they are water soluble, so avoid even these when you can.

What about buying pressure-treated lumber for outdoor use from your local lumberyard? Until 2003 in the United States, this lumber was treated with the highly toxic chromated copper arsenic (CCA); this chemical has been banned from use in children's playgrounds in the European Union and is being voluntarily phased out in the United States in association with the Environmental Protection Agency, but it is still commonly used in the United Kingdom so you'll have to be vigilant to avoid it. Now pressure-treated timber is more frequently preserved with the less toxic alkaline copper quaternary (ACQ, made up of copper, an insecticide, and a fungicide) or copper azole (CA, marketed under the Wolmanized brand in the United States and the Tanelith brand across Europe). Timber treated with any of these chemicals should be used only for patios, decks, and walkways and should not be used where it may become a component of food, animal feed, or beehives; it should also not be burned, composted, or turned into mulch.

Colouring your wood

Adding a lick of paint to your garden can be a cheap and easy way to spruce up a tired-looking shed, fence, or wall. The problem is as soon as you apply your chemical paints and stains to untreated timber, you are preventing it from being added to the compost heap at the end of its life; it's heading for the landfill again. It's a bit of a quandary, really, as one of the main reasons to paint something is to prolong its life or usefulness in a scheme.

The simplest solution is to try to choose a product that will still allow the timber to be safely composted at the end of its life. Welsh family-run company Rendona produces three main ranges of exterior paint. Their environmentally friendly paints and pigments can be applied to different surfaces such as wood, garden timber, concrete render, brick, and stonework, and there is a good range of colours to choose from, including muted tones and brights. In the United States, YOLO Colorhouse offers an excellent range of environmentally friendly exterior paints with no added chemicals or solvents.

Plastic lumber

One of the most popular new materials to emerge in the landscape design sector is plastic lumber. Manufacturers claim it saves hardwood forests, cuts down on maintenance, prevents termite attack, and is a good use for recycled plastic waste. The problem is that the plastic lumber industry is susceptible to greenwashing, and plastic lumber products can vary from an admirable 100 percent post-consumer recycled content to a horrific 100 percent virgin plastic resin. It can be difficult for a consumer to work out which is the most sustainable product.

When choosing plastic lumber, you need to consider three points: What are the materials used? How much is recycled content? Will I be able to reuse or recycle it at the end of its life?

MATERIAL CHOICES. No plastic is environmentally benign, but buyers should choose polyethylene over polystyrene or polyvinyl chloride (PVC). Try also to avoid fibreglass content (which is sometimes added to increase the load-bearing capacity).

RECYCLED CONTENT. Try to choose a product with at least 50 percent post-consumer content.

REUSE. Polyethylene is very easy to recycle, so it can be reused after its intended life as plastic lumber. Composite products are harder to recycle effectively, so try to avoid plastic lumber with additives, such as other plastics, fibreglass, or wood fibre.

GREEN TIP **If you choose to treat your timber, try raw linseed oil. Or get an environmentally responsible exterior paint from Rendona in the United Kingdom (www.rendona.co.uk) or YOLO Colorhouse in the United States (www.yolocolorhouse.com).**

Do not grow food on the site of an old deck, since the lumber was probably treated with the highly toxic chemical chromated copper arsenic (CCA).

Rethinking the Lawn

Now that lawns are a staple feature of most domestic gardens, it can be easy to forget that they were once the preserve of the super-rich. Few people could afford to own land that was not used to produce food, so a lawn was the ultimate show of wealth. At that time, grass had to be cut with a hand scythe, so even a modest-sized lawn required a permanent gardening staff. With the invention of the lawn mower and the development of new strains of turf, lawns may have become easier to maintain, but they are still one of the greediest elements in any garden: demanding mowing, scarifying or aerating, fertilizers, pesticides, and enormous quantities of water.

In her 1994 book *The Lawn: A History of an American Obsession*, Virginia Scott Jenkins argues that "American front lawns are a symbol of man's control of, or superiority over, his environment." This suppression of the natural habit of turfgrass is exactly why people criticize the sustainability of the lawn. By keeping the lawn cut short, we never allow the vegetation to reproduce or mature as it would naturally. But do we have to give up lawns entirely? Perhaps there is a way to make lawns more eco.

A brief history of the lawn

The first lawns were fashionable in late eighteenth-century France and England. One of the earliest examples of the use of lawn in garden design was when landscape architect Andre Le Notre designed small lawn areas for the Palace of Versailles. This new trend was soon adopted by wealthy British landowners who found that it suited their reliably rainy climate.

The U.S. love affair with lawns is a little more complex. It began with wealthy homeowners copying the look of English estates in the eighteenth century. Not until after the Civil War did middle-class homeowners begin to adopt the lawn in swathes. The widespread U.S tradition of having a front garden laid to lawn may in fact have originated from a simple misunderstanding. Architects' plans often showed the house in a simple plot surrounded by a low lawn, but this was not a fashion choice—it was simply due to the fact that drawing in shrubs and vegetation would have taken more time (and therefore cost more to illustrate) and would have hidden the architectural detailing on the plans.

It can be said that Frederick Law Olmsted cemented the U.S obsession with the lawn when he drew up the designs for Riverside (one of the first planned suburban communities in the United States) in 1868. As a reaction against the terraced rows of housing that dominated Europe during the nineteeth century, Olmstead stipulated that each house be set back 30 feet from the road, with a front lawn that would flow seamlessly from one neighbour to the next. For middle-class homeowners, the idea that they too could adopt the parkland style of the English landscape tradition (so popular with the most wealthy Americans and Brits) must have been very appealing.

Unfortunately, the widespread adoption of this front garden parkland style is what has made the U.S. relationship with the lawn so troubled. The success of this approach relied on each individual homeowner maintaining an immaculate lawn—and this brought social pressures into play. With no boundaries, walls, or fences to offer privacy in the front garden, anyone who had a different idea for their front garden would meet stiff resistance from neighbours.

Another important factor in the rise of the lawn was a growing interest in golf. In the late nineteenth and early twentieth century, the USDA, the U.S. Golf Association, and the Garden Clubs of America jointly spread the front lawn ethic throughout the United States. They reinforced the social pressure of the perfect lawn through competitions for landscaping—and they shamed neighbours into compliance. The social pressure to maintain an immaculate lawn still remains in many parts of the United States, and some properties have lawn requirements written into their deeds. Homeowners worried about the impact a different front garden style will have on their house prices might still be tempted to exert a bit of peer pressure on neighbours who have more progressive ideas for their front yards, but gradually opinions are changing.

In defence of the lawn

The anti-lawn movement has been around for several decades now, encouraging gardeners to replace their lawns with crops or flowers—but if you really like your lawn, you don't have to take such a radical step. Modern lawns do have their uses; they are great for recreation and they make a soft surface for kids' play areas, football pitches, and tennis courts. And as large areas of permeable ground, lawns can make great flood defences.

GREEN TIP **Limit lawn to key design areas, rather than using it as an inexpensive fill material. Mixed plantings are more interesting to look at, easier to maintain, and have a proven benefit to wildlife. Stop thinking of lawn as the standard ground plane for a garden and think about it as a feature—to be used carefully and only when appropriate. An area of lawn might be important in an accurate historical restoration of a garden, for example, or for a compact soft play area close to the house.**

To make it more eco, stop applying pesticides and fertilizers to your lawn, and stop irrigating it. Try a manual push mower or a battery-powered mower to minimize energy use. Consider a mulching mower to recycle grass clippings as mulch. Include some nitrogen-fixing plants in your planting, such as clover.

Lawns are a sustainability paradox, but perhaps the idea of a lawn is not the problem. The materials we choose and the way we manage our lawns might yet supply a solution. Lawns don't have to be immaculate, velvety carpets of monoculture. They can be diverse, hardy plantings that do all the jobs we need a lawn to do without costing the earth.

There are a number of simple and significant changes that you can make to the way you manage your lawn that will make it easier and cheaper to look after. First, stop using weed killers and artificial fertilizers. This will allow native plants to return to the lawn: wildflowers such as violets, clovers, bugle, and thymes. At the same time, stop irrigating your lawn. The colonizing wildflowers have a far greater drought tolerance than the grasses that make up a traditional lawn, and you will immediately see less scorching and browning in the summer.

Raise the blades on your lawn mower to 3.5 to 5 cm (1 to 2 in) to cut your grass a little longer. You won't have to mow your lawn as frequently and it will help to keep your lawn looking green in warm, dry weather. Grass helps to retain soil moisture, so raising the blades will make a noticeable difference.

Alternative lawns

If you have your heart set on a lawn for aesthetic reasons, why not consider using low-growing plants to give the effect of a lawn (that is, a well-managed area allowing a view of surrounding border plants) without such firm demands on your time or resources? Following are descriptions of some plants that can fill the bill quite nicely.

CHAMOMILE. Before ryegrass took over as the plant of choice, lawns were made of chamomile. Chamomile is a low-growing aromatic herb that is drought tolerant and tough enough to be walked on. The low-growing variety 'Trenague' knits together to form a lush green sward that does not require mowing. Although Chamomile lawns are pretty much restricted to sandy, free-draining soil (and probably would not be up to much as a football pitch), they make an excellent alternative that does not turn brown in dry weather. In fact, since Buckingham Palace boasts a fine chamomile lawn, you could say it's fit for a queen!

CLOVER. For gardeners with a heavy clay soil, clover makes a great alternative lawn. With its long taproots, clover can access water deep down in the sub-soil and stay green throughout even the driest summers. Clover will thrive on a poor soil, and as a bonus for dog lovers, it even tolerates

Grasscycling, or mulch mowing, is the natural recycling of grass cuttings. Instead of collecting and removing your clippings each time you mow the lawn, you simply leave them on the surface of the lawn as a nutritious mulch. Grasscycling originated on golf courses and is a great way to supply the nutrients turf needs to stay green, lush, and healthy.

The key to grasscycling is to keep your mower blade sharp, never cut more than a third off the height of your lawn, and never mow the grass when it is wet. Because the clippings are small, they will disappear into the lawn without clumping, to leave you with a neat, tidy finish.

Don't be put off by rumours that grasscycling can cause thatch buildup. It's simply not true (it's the shoots and roots that form a thatch, not the clippings). Mulch mowing recycles the nutrients exactly where you need them and cuts down on the time you need to spend looking after your lawn and the green waste you generate, all the while achieving a neat and tidy look. It's a gardener's dream!

the odd spray of urine without bleaching yellow. Clover also provides food for bees with its blossoms, and it fixes nitrogen in your soil. Dutch white clover (*Trifolium repens*) is the variety to look for, as this is the low-growing, spreading perennial.

ACAENA MICROPHYLLA. Another good plant for poor soil is *Acaena microphylla*. With its glaucous colouring and copper-coloured burrs it quickly knits together to form a dense horizontal planting. Although traditionally grown in thin, well-drained soils, this can succeed equally well in heavy, semi-shaded clay. Avoid *Acaena* if you have pets, as the burrs can become a pain.

THYME. Thyme is a classic choice for a sunny garden with free-draining soil. Drought tolerant and low growing, your thyme lawn will require just a once-over with the shears every year to keep it looking neat and tidy. Wild thyme (*Thymus polytrichus*) is a good choice, or you can try interweaving *Thymus porlock* and woolly thyme, *Thymus pseudolanuginosus*, for a more painterly effect.

LEPTINELLA SQUALIDA OR MOSS. In a shady spot, you might want to take a leaf out of the book of Japanese garden designers and consider a moss. Alternatively, *Leptinella squalida*, a creeping evergreen from New Zealand, makes a great alternative lawn because it only grows to a height of 2.5 cm (1 in).

(top left) Why not consider laying wildflower turf rather than a conventional monoculture turf? The pregrown meadow in a roll will act as a weed mulch while the meadow establishes and will only need cutting once a year.

(top right) Try interweaving *Thymus porlock* and woolly thyme, *Thymus pseudolanuginosus*, for a more painterly effect.

(right) Clover is brilliant for biodiversity (especially for bees, who need all the help they can get at the moment). Clover is really rich in nutrients and can be used as a green manure to regenerate the soil.

Artificial grass

Advances in technology mean that artificial lawns are finally start-ing to look convincingly naturalistic—and many U.S. states now offer a rebate for the conversion of water-greedy turf lawns to fake lawns or synthetic turf. Fake grass can cost up to ten times as much as a turf lawn to install, but since there are no real maintenance costs, you would break even with a fake lawn after only ten years. But is there any way an environmentally conscious gardener can justify its use in the garden?

Fake grass is made from crude oil and is not biodegradable. Although it can be recycled, yet more energy would be required to convert it into something new. However, natural turf lawns are also very greedy consumers of resources, where fake grass doesn't have to be watered, fertilized, or mowed. So does removing mower emissions, reducing chemical runoff, and reducing water use and noise pollution offset the resources required to produce and dispose of this material?

Another factor to consider is the effect of the lawn on biodiversity and the garden environment. Obviously, fake turf does not create a rich habitat for wildlife. It does not photosynthesize and therefore does not absorb CO_2 from the atmosphere. In addition, because it doesn't tran-

(left) You can now get fake grass with a nondirectional weave and up to four different coloured "blades" for a more naturalistic look. Lazy Lawn

(right) Fake grass allows designers to create neat stepping-stone effects that would be very high maintenance in a growing lawn, as can be seen in this Chelsea Garden Show design from Lazy Lawn. Lazy Lawn

GREEN TIP Don't buy teak garden furniture. Look for furniture made from recycled or reclaimed materials. If you must colour it, use a water-based product.

spire, gardens lose out on the beneficial insulating and cooling qualities of a natural turf lawn. Fake grass is made from polyethelene, which can get pretty hot in midsummer. Contrast this with the cool feel of natural grass under your feet and you may instantly go off the idea.

Sustainable Furniture

There is no excuse for buying teak garden furniture (even if it is sustainably harvested) when so much environmental damage is done shipping it many miles. Buy recycled garden furniture, or furniture made from reclaimed materials. In the United Kingdom, choose English oak from local managed woodlands, or if you must have teak, choose furniture made from salvaged or recycled wood. In the United States, western red cedar and cypress are excellent choices. Furniture made from recycled or reclaimed materials is clearly the most sustainable option, as these materials are already in circulation.

Avoid oil-based paints and stains. Choose wood that is suitable for outdoor use without treatment, such as oak, sweet chestnut, larch, western red cedar, or Douglas fir. If you must colour your wood, choose water-based products so that any wooden furniture can be recycled or composted at the end of its useful life.

5

Choosing Materials for Boundaries and Structures

Walls and boundaries define a garden.

In towns and cities, they enclose and protect; in the wider landscape, they frame views and stamp a pattern on the land. Many areas of the world have a local boundary or walling style that defines the area. In Cumbria, dry-stone walls make a jigsaw of the landscape, flint walls dominate an area of East Anglia, and the creamy yellow sandstone of the Cotswolds is recognizable far outside the United Kingdom. Think adobe walls in New Mexico, picket fences in Maine, and split-rail fences in North Carolina.

Building a boundary shows long-term vision for a landscape. It provides privacy, shade, and shelter, insulates a landscape from noise, and dictates movement. For a long time brick or stone garden walls were the ultimate status symbol, but cheaper fences and hedges soon came to dominate gardens around the world. When sustainability enters in, a new set of choices about materials awaits us.

Hedges

Planting a hedge is probably the cheapest and most ecological way to create a garden boundary. There are a whole range of hedging options to choose from, depending on the height, depth, amount of maintenance, and level of formality you require. Yew, holly, hornbeam, beech, and mixed natives are some of the classic favourites.

Yew is a classic choice for dividing the garden into rooms. It gives a dense evergreen structure to your garden, glossy even in the depth of winter, and requires trimming only once a year. Yew tolerates both sun and shade but is slow to establish and hates standing water, so it does best in a well-drained site. Another choice evergreen is holly, which forms lush walls and has traditionally been popular for mazes.

Hornbeam and beech, although deciduous, hold onto their autumn leaves until the new leaves push them off in the spring. This semi-evergreen quality makes them another classic choice for garden hedges; their strong winter structure harmonizes with the rusts and golden brown tones of the winter garden. Fast growing and inexpensive to install, beech and hornbeam are useful hedging materials for gardens big and small.

Mixed native hedges are the final classic choice to consider. An infinitely variable combination of fruit trees, roses, and other flowering

PROJECT   Make a living willow fedge

Willow is a material gardeners will come across time and time again. Fast growing and quick to take root, even from a cut stem, willow is a great sustainable resource that can be used to make living fences, or fedges—as well as retaining structures, arches, and arbours.

The best time to make your own fedge is in the winter when the willow is dormant. You can order bundles of living willow from your local willow farm (if you are cutting the willow yourself, go for about 5cm diameter and height to suit your purpose). First place a series of willow rods into the ground at intervals of 2 to 3 m (about 6.5 to 10 ft) to create your fence posts. Then string a guideline between these posts to indicate the desired height of your finished fedge. Next, plant half your rods at a 45-degree angle 25 to 40 cm (1 to 1.3 ft)

apart. Once you reach the end of your fedge, plant the remaining willow rods so that they slant the opposite way – to create a diamond pattern. Make sure each rod extends at least 30 cm (about 1 ft) below the soil level to allow a good root system to develop.

I like to cut down on weeding by planting through a geotextile weed barrier; if I have particularly thick willow rods, I make a guide hole with a metal rod before attempting to push the willow into the ground. Once all your rods have been planted, weave the rods together to hold them in place, bending them horizontally along the guide wire. In a windy spot, you can give your new living hedge a bit more security with flexible rubber ties or loosely tied garden string.

and fruiting plants can be left to thicken up naturally or laid to form a neat woven hedge. Mixed native hedges are particularly important for wildlife because they include such a diverse range of plants, providing shelter and nesting sites for birds and mammals. The inclusion of a mixed native hedge is often a planning requirement in rural areas; consult your local planning officer for advice on the best combination of plants for your area.

Many gardeners avoid hedges because they fear that they take too long to grow, or take up too much space and need regular maintenance. The truth is that hedges are one of the most versatile boundaries available to a garden designer, and you can quickly grow a single-row hornbeam hedge as narrow as 30 cm (about 1 ft).

GREEN TIP **Plant a hedge to create a garden boundary that's economical and friendly to wildlife. Yew and holly are classic evergreen choices; hornbeam and beech are faster-growing deciduous choices. Use mixed natives to provide shelter and nesting sites for birds and mammals.**

Fences

Wood is often a good choice for fences and structures in the garden, especially if it comes from a local managed forest or coppice. In the

(top left) Yew hedges can take a while to grow, but the wait is worth it.

(top right) Hedges of box, yew, and hornbeam at graduated heights provide privacy and shelter without an oppressive sense of enclosure. Garden Collection/Derek Harris

(bottom left) All hedges encourage biodiversity, but mixed hedges are particularly important for local wildlife.

(bottom right) *Salix viminalis* (basket willow or common osier) is the best choice for living willow structures; you can buy rods of willow from your local grower at very low cost.

last chapter we looked at the sustainability issues surrounding wood in some detail, and the same principles apply here. Remember that even sustainably sourced tropical hardwoods are not very eco because of the hundreds of miles they have to travel before they reach your garden. Reclaimed tropical hardwoods, black locust, or green oak are a much better choice for landscaping because they are already in the country. Other materials to consider include bamboo, woven willow or hazel hurdles—even old scaffold boards and roofing battens.

Local or reclaimed wood

Trees managed through coppicing are one of the most sustainable sources of wood. Coppicing is a traditional method of woodland management that can be used to produce a steady supply of stakes, poles, and other timber without the need to replant.

Coppicing has proved itself as a sustainable way to manage temperate forests in the United Kingdom and the United States. A wide variety of trees can be coppiced, including alder, birch, oak, and poplar, but the most popular choices are willow, hazel (hazelnut), and sweet chestnut, as they grow most quickly and can be harvested regularly. In coppiced woodland, the trees are cut back to near ground level and allowed to regenerate from stumps (known as stools). Lots of new shoots will grow up from the stool and these will be ready for harvesting in just a few years.

Traditionally, a coppiced woodland is harvested in rotation so that wood is always available for use. The period of time between harvests depends on the speed of growth of each material as well as on the eventual use of the timber. Short rotation coppice (SRC) is usually densely planted, high-yielding varieties of willow or poplar harvested on a three-year cycle. Hazel is usually grown on a seven-to-ten-year rotation. Sweet chestnut can be harvested anywhere between five years for trugs and fifteen years for fence poles, although fifteen years is the standard. The slowest-growing timbers, such as oak and ash, need a far longer twenty-five-to-thirty-five-year cycle between harvests but are not planted as densely to allow for the longer period of growth.

Few large-scale commercial coppice stands remain in the United Kingdom, although sweet chestnut is grown as fencing material in parts of East Sussex and Kent, and a large number of willow and hazel growers use pollarding (a similar method) to grow withies for weaving hurdles and baskets. Understanding of the economic benefits of coppicing

GREEN TIP **Choose local, reclaimed, or recycled wood for the most sustainable fences.**

Woods suitable for coppicing include beech, hazel, birch, sweet chestnut, poplar, hornbeam, ash, alder, willow, and oak. Willow and hazel can be woven into elegant hurdles, while sweet chestnut makes excellent rustic fences and posts. For a more chunky finish, or for the clean lines of sawn wood, locally grown oak would make an exquisite choice.

Coppiced plants are cut right back to the base each winter. Lots of new shoots regrow for the stump or stool the following spring. Jane Sebire

is gaining momentum, and grants may be available for the restoration of coppice woodland.

You can weave your own hurdles for fences, raised beds, and borders using freshly harvested or dried hazel or willow. If the wood is dried, soak it in cold water for three or four days to make it flexible enough for weaving. Hazel is excellent for weaving plant supports such as frames for peonies and obelisques for climbing plants. It also makes a lovely garden plant in multi-stem form, and the purple-leaved variety makes an excellent backdrop to any border.

Fences can also be made from recycled materials such as scaffold boards or roofing battens. Talk to local contractors and scaffolding suppliers or visit a reclaimed building materials supplier to track these down. Just be sure to avoid old treated wood, which is best regarded as hazardous waste since it's likely to have been treated with chromated copper arsenic (CCA).

(top) Locally grown FSC oak is turned into fence posts, panels, and trellises. Quercus Oak Fencing

(bottom) Picket fences have been popular in the United States since the seventeenth century. Many people still view a low white picket fence as a symbol of the ideal middle-class suburban life.

(top) Coppiced wood is worth considering for rustic pergolas, fences, and retaining walls as well as plant supports like these at Pete Woollam's Hough Lane Garden in Cheshire, England. It ticks lots of sustainability boxes and is a renewable material, too. Jane Sebire

(bottom) Recycled timber, such as these old scaffold boards used in a display garden at the Chelsea Flower Show designed by Kate Gould, can make a very stylish boundary. Kate Gould Gardens

Bamboo

Bamboo is an extremely fast growing building material. It's durable and renewable, with a proven vernacular tradition, but is it sustainable? Some people claim bamboo is such a good substitute for timber products that it could help to prevent the destruction of ancient forests for wood.

Let's look at the facts. Bamboo requires few resources to grow, can be grown on poor soil, and can be useful in stabilizing slopes. Fast-growing species of bamboo often reach their full height in one year and their full strength within three. Unlike coppiced wood, bamboo will not regrow from cut stems, but it spreads quickly by runners so it is self-sustaining. But in gardens, bamboo runners may be as much a curse as a blessing. Bamboo is known to be an invasive plant, so there are concerns about commercial bamboo plantations encroaching on land that is important for other uses or for biodiversity preservation.

The species of bamboo grown and harvested for building materials are not the same species that pandas and other wildlife use as a food source. At present, most commercially available bamboo is harvested from the Pacific Rim. The environmental issues raised by the need to transport this material halfway around the world makes it hard to justify bamboo as a sustainable material. Luckily, bamboo grows in a wide range of climates, and if a local network of growers could be established, bamboo could yet fulfill its potential as a sustainable building material.

Walls

Most walls use cement, either in the form of mortar, concrete blocks, or cement-based render (a durable material applied to the outside of block-built walls). One of the most effective ways to improve the green credentials of a garden is to exclude cement from its construction, but this is easier said than done.

Bamboo varieties grown for building include *Bambusa burmanica*, *Dendrocalamus giganteus* and *D. membranaceus*, *Guadua chacoensis*, and *Thyrsostachys siamensis*.

Building blocks

Concrete blocks are a popular choice in construction. Large but light-weight, they allow structures to be put up with ever-increasing speed. For the sustainable gardener, always trying to reduce the amount of concrete and cement in your landscape, they can represent a real temptation. The environmental impact of concrete can be mitigated with

(top left) Dry-stone walls are built without mortar and were traditionally built with the stones turned up when clearing land for agriculture, but they can be used in contemporary gardens too, as can be seen in this show garden from the Tatton Park Flower Show in 2004. Decorative Aggregates

(top right) Hempcrete blocks are among the new lightweight alternatives to stone or fired bricks. Lime Technology

(bottom left) Mortar-free walls don't have to be limited to stone, but they are neatest in stone. This wall at the Oase Garden in the Netherlands is contructed from stacked bricks and adds a romantic feel to the garden. Jane Sebire

(bottom right) Honeycomb blocks interlock to reduce the amount of mortar required. Natural Building Technologies

GREEN TIP **Consider honeycomb blocks of fired clay, hempcrete blocks, super adobe, or dry stone as an eco-friendly alternative to cement building blocks.**

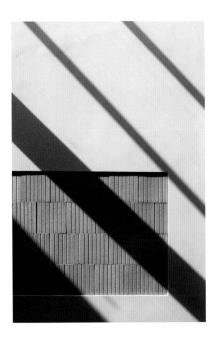

Lime render can be applied over Ziegel blocks to make a wall with impeccable green credentials. Natural Building Technologies

cement substitutions such as pulverised fuel ash or ground granulated blast furnace slag, and through the use of recycled aggregates, as mentioned in chapter 3, but there are some cement-free alternatives to consider, too.

Honeycomb blocks of fired clay require 30 percent less energy to produce than concrete blocks. Their cellular structure gives them the strength to be considered as a serious alternative to concrete blocks for most applications. These honeycomb blocks—known as Ziegel or thermoplan—are assembled by interlocking the dry blocks with a reduced amount of mortar pointing. The honeycomb structure traps air within the clay block, making them excellent thermal insulators. The hollow structure also reduces their weight, which in turn reduces associated transport energy demands and makes construction go more quickly. Although these clay building blocks still require high-temperature kilns for production, they result in nearly two-thirds less CO_2 than the production of concrete blocks and are well worth considering.

Hempcrete blocks are relatively new to the market. Manufactured from hemp blended with a lime and cement binder, they are suitable for low-carbon construction due to the blocks' ability to sequester carbon from the environment. Lightweight and easy to use, hempcrete blocks are fully recyclable and biodegradable. Another alternative, earthbag construction—the use of long fabric bags filled with earth, gravel, or other waste material to construct walls and buildings—is gaining popularity because it's cheap and easy, and it uses local materials. When the bags are filled with moist earth, the material is known as super adobe.

The render applied to the outside of block-built walls was traditionally lime-based. But for many years, lime was abandoned in favour of cement-based renders, which would set quickly even in cold or wet conditions. Now lime is back in favour once again because of its flexibility and eco-credentials. Lime is not as brittle as cement and tolerates some movement. It suffers less from cracks than a cement-based render and even has the ability to heal small cracks itself as water dissolves free lime in the render.

Brick

Sustainability issues surrounding fired brick were discussed in chapter 3. Unfired mud bricks (adobe) and compressed earth blocks are a good alternative where a load-bearing structure is not required. They require very little energy to manufacture, and new formulations are being developed all the time. Earthen bricks can be stacked and mortared together in a wall, like using fired bricks.

Cob

Cob is a mixture of clay, sand, and straw that can be shaped into structures using hands and feet. Building with cob, adobe, or rammed earth is a great example of a closed loop system. The building materials are usually available on (or close to) the site and would otherwise be considered waste materials; this keeps costs down and reduces transport miles. And the structure is fully recyclable at the end of its life.

Earthen buildings have been around since the Stone Age, but there is also a long tradition of building garden walls out of cob. Cob walls were particularly sought after for kitchen gardens because of their ability to act as thermal regulators. Earth walls absorb heat from the sun during the day and release this stored energy as the temperature drops. This creates a microclimate perfect for growing fruit such as peaches and apricots.

The main material required for building with cob is clay subsoil, a material usually regarded as waste. Landscapers and builders often pay to have this "waste product" taken away, so you will find it easy to get ahold of—even if there is not suitable subsoil on your site. To this clay subsoil you add sand or angular aggregate (often found on-site) and long, dry fibres such as straw, heather, or rushes. The addition of fibres gives strength and flexibility to the cob that allows for some natural movement and prevents cracking. The straw allows the cob mixture to regulate moisture and will soak up excess moisture in the wall, while the air trapped in the hollow stems of the straw will help with heat and sound insulation.

Earthen construction is one of the cheapest construction methods available to the gardener since it uses free, local (on-site) materials and eliminates the need to spend money getting rid of subsoil from the site.

GREEN TIP Source your straw direct from a local farmer. It will be freshest and cheapest if you buy your straw around the time of the harvest—in late summer or early autumn. Make sure your straw is dry, as wet, rotting fibres will not add anything to the strength of a wall.

(top left) A stem wall protects cob walls from water damage and should be built at least 450 mm (1.5 ft) high unless you are building your cob structure directly onto bedrock. Garden Collection/Andrew Lawson

(top right) Cob is a mixture of clay, sand, and straw that can be used to build walls and buildings. Lime render offers extra protection from the elements while allowing your cob structure to breathe. Cob walls can take a long time to fully dry out, so external rendering should be postponed until at least twelve months after completion. Clayworks/Katy Bryce

(center right) Rammed earth walls make an attractive backdrop to plantings and make use of materials already on-site, as in this Chelsea show garden designed by Sarah Price.

(bottom) Cob walls were a traditional feature of eighteenth-century kitchen gardens, and they create a perfect microclimate for wall-trained fruit. Garden Collection/Andrew Lawson

PROJECT Build with cob

Traditionally, cob structures have been built directly on top of the earth. This method succeeds best where a thin layer of chalky soil covers solid bedrock. In areas of soft clay, you would be wise to use a stem wall. In general, the key to longevity for cob is to provide a waterproof "hat and boots" to protect the structure from water damage. At the base of the wall, footings support the structure below ground level and a 450-mm (1.5-ft) stem wall prevents splashback and rising damp. At the top of the wall, a wide thatch, slate, turf, or tile roof will protect the structure, providing it has a wide enough overhang. When planning a cap or roof for your garden wall, you should design an overhang of at least 300 mm (1 ft) so that water can be shed clear of the walls.

To test that you have your cob mixture just right, make a ball the size of a fist and drop it to the ground from waist height. If the ball crumbles upon impact, you need to add more clay. If the ball squashes flat like a pancake, you need to add more sand. If the ball stays in a ball, you have a good mix.

Building a cob wall requires time, since it needs to be built in lifts—sections of between 300 and 600 mm (1 to 2 ft) in height. If you try to build your cob wall too quickly, it will slump or collapse and you will have to start again. After you build each lift, you must allow the cob to dry out for three to four days. Once it is hard, but still workable, you can trim your wall to shape using a spade or saw, and then use an old cricket or baseball bat to compress the wall by whacking it from the side.

You will need to protect your cob walls from the elements and help keep the drying rate consistent during construction. This is most easily achieved using a simple tarpaulin, anchored with rocks or logs. If you are not removing your tarpaulin every few days to work on the structure, you will need to put a layer of straw or hessian between the structure and the tarpaulin to absorb the condensation that will form on the inside of the tarp.

Labour is the only real cost. However, it is worth bearing in mind that earthen structures are time consuming to build, and there is a limit to how much you can adapt the aesthetic of the structure without compromising its longevity, so it may not be suitable for all styles of garden design.

Dry stone

One of the best ways to avoid using cement in your garden is to use dry-stone walls. Dry-stone walls are some of the most beautiful walls around, and they score highly in terms of sustainability, too. A well-built dry-stone wall needs no mortar; instead, the individual stones lock together, gaining additional strength as they settle. Dry-stone

PROJECT   Construct a Devon bank

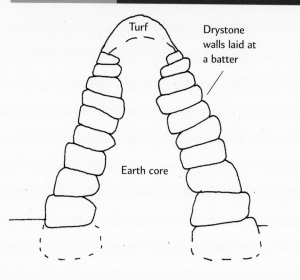

Devon banks are hollow dry-stone walls with an earthern core that can be used as a type of living boundary.

Devon banks, also known as Cornish hedges (and Clawd or Cloddiau in Wales), are stone-faced earth banks with turf, wildflowers, or hedges growing along the top. The English county of Devon has many miles of these ancient and distinctive hedges which are often more than 800 years old. They are a simple, self-sustaining ecosystem that can easily be incorporated into your own garden design. The key to these hollow dry-stone walls is the clay-based earth core. The combination of stone and clay keeps the soil cool, encouraging condensation and preventing water loss, while the low fertility keeps weeds at bay.

When you build a Devon bank, make the base as wide as the eventual height—so for a 2 m (6 ft) high wall, space your parallel walls at least 2 m (6 ft) apart. Start with your largest stones at the bottom and fill the void with compacted gritty clay. As you add each subsequent layer of stone (300 mm or 1 ft between courses is about right), lay them slightly closer together so that the overall shape of the wall follows a concave batter (receding upward slope). A 2 m (6 ft) wall should gradually narrow to only 0.6 m (2 ft) at the top.

The theory is that the stones hold the earth (not vice versa) and that the batter means the wall creates less wind turbulence and directs any rainwater into the earth core. This earth core is vital to the success of the Devon bank because it gives the wall extra weight and entices plants to take root in the cracks and crevices, which further binds the wall together. Devon banks can support a diverse planting scheme, from hawthorn and wild roses to ferns, turf, and wildflowers.

walls are suited to both straight lines and curves, and all the nooks and crannies are soon colonized by plants and animals, so they are great for biodiversity.

Dry-stone walls are a traditional British construction technique, widely used by farmers in Scotland, Yorkshire, and Cumbria. The technique has been adapted for use in garden designs—for water features, walls, and even furniture. Dry-stone construction is less common in the United States (although it has been in use since colonial times), but there is a growing interest in this technique and British experts have started to offer dry-stack master classes in the states. Dry-stone construction is also becoming more popular in Canada; the Dry Stone Wall Association of Canada was founded in 2000.

Seek the advice of a local expert if you are planning a dry-stone wall, as stones and styles vary. Be wary of including too much dry-stone construction in urban, built-up areas as it can look very out of place. And if you're building a really long dry-stone wall, it's a good idea to put in holes for badgers to go through—they're the biggest destroyer of dry-stone walls as they just dig through when they can't find a hole.

Gabions

Gabions are essentially metal cages made from steel mesh. They have been used in civil engineering projects since medieval times. They are an inexpensive way to construct retaining walls and can also be used to create freestanding structures, seats, and even water features. From a sustainability standpoint, they have both pluses and minuses. Steel requires intense heat for production, but the steel used in gabions is usually recycled from scrap, which reduces these energy demands by nearly three-fourths. On the positive side, gabions are compact (flat packed) and light to transport, which cuts down on transport energy, and once assembled they can be filled with waste or recycled materials.

Wood

Wood can be used to construct low retaining walls. These can work in a way similar to gabions, using sheer weight to hold back the earth; or they can be built like a fence with supporting posts at regular intervals faced with thinner boards. For taller structures, metal rods can be used to secure the stack of wood.

Please, please, please avoid using reclaimed railway sleepers (railroad ties). These will have been treated with creosote (now banned from sale in the European Union) and it will leach out and contaminate your garden soil. In hot weather, oily residues can seep out of the sleepers. New untreated oak sleepers are a more sustainable choice.

GREEN TIP Avoid using old sleepers in a garden; they will have been treated with creosote, which will ooze out of the wood in hot weather and contaminate your soil.

Any abundant local waste material can be used to fill gabions.

(top left) Gabions filled with pine cones provide a great habitat for beneficial insects. Garden Collection/Neil Sutherland

(top right) You can fill gabions with any abundant waste material. Garden designer Mark Stapleford has used all sorts of items reclaimed from the garden, from Victorian clay lawn edging to stones. Mark Stapleford Landscape Design

(center right) Use whatever you have to hand to fill gabions. Empty bottles are perfect. Garden Collection/Neil Sutherland

(bottom right) Gabions are the ultimate in design for disassembly as all the components can be reused over and over again. Try making a bench, a stool, a retaining wall, or steps. Mark Stapleford Landscape Design

Bio-engineering for Erosion Control

We have already seen how useful willow can be for a living hedge because of its ability to root from freshly cut rods. Bio-engineering takes this principle one step further, using living structures to retain slopes with densely rooted living plantings. Rods or stakes of willow, dogwood, or poplar cut from a sustainable coppice are a light and dextrous material, and they can be relied on to strike roots within days and weeks. This method of erosion control has been in use for thousands of years around the globe, and there are several methods worth considering in the greener garden.

The simplest method is to use sections of branches (stripped of shoots and leaves) planted directly into the bank. As with the living hedge, pilot holes may be required in harder soils. Choose rods 2.5 cm (1 in) or more in diameter over the entire length and 0.5 to 1 m (1 to 3 ft) long. You can insert these by hand or with the help of a mallet. Live rods are a great way to stabilize slopes because of their dual action: the rods provide initial stabilization (in a way similar to steel reinforcing rods in concrete), the roots stabilize the soil, and sprouting leaves help to deflect rain and thus protect the soil from erosion.

Variations on this method include wattle and brush mattresses, where woven mats of live branches are staked to the slope; fascines or faggots, where bundles of branches are buried lengthways in trenches along the contours of the slope; brush layering, where branches are placed into the slope and backfilled with earth; and live crib walls. Another popular way to manage the erosion of slopes uses long "sausages" of netting stuffed with straw to capture sediment. Lightweight and durable but inexpensive, straw wattles are flexible enough to be used on uneven or rocky surfaces.

Traditional Methods of Landscape Construction

Many areas of landscape construction have seen a resurgence of interest in traditional methods. Much of this revival stems from the practical problem of working on a garden where the only point of access is through the house, but traditional skills for moving heavy objects without heavy machinery will always come in handy.

Think carefully about the methods and machinery you choose when building a garden. Traditional methods are often the simplest, easi-

GREEN TIP **If you have a steep slope where you need to control erosion, consider using gabions filled with stone, or live rods that eventually form dense roots to hold the soil.**

Plants to use for bio-engineering

A number of plants can be used for erosion control, although the most sustainable choice will be a locally grown species. Here are some favourite plant choices:

- *Cornus sericea* (often lower success rate than willows)
- *Populus balsamifera*
- *Salix geyeriana*
- *Salix hookeriana*
- *Salix hookeriana* var. *piperi*
- *Salix lucida*
- *Salix scouleriana*
- *Salix sitchensis*

est, and greenest choice—allowing you to avoid the time, hassle, and expense of hiring in machinery. A simple rule of thumb is to use mechanized equipment only when it offers a genuine advantage over people power, and when in doubt to choose the lightest available machinery. On sensitive sites, small equipment is often more effective than heavy machinery and is less damaging to the all important soil structure.

Where fuel is required, try to pick the most sustainable option by choosing fuel made from a waste resource. Ask how much energy is returned on energy invested. Remember, not all heavy equipment is unsustainable. A crane can lift heavy materials over protected parts of a site in lieu of many trips with wheelbarrows and trucks. Whether this is considered sustainable will depend on the energy efficiency of the machine as well as the importance of protecting site features.

The pole sling was widely used in the United States and Europe until the 1880s and is still a common and energy-efficient choice in Asia for moving heavy objects. A pole sling uses two long poles and a sling to distribute the weight of an object. This technique is very useful for gardeners, as any scaffold pole, sapling trunk, or even a couple of simple 2×4 lengths of timber can be used. A pole sling is especially good for lifting irregular objects, such as large rocks, because the poles can be used to keep your body a comfortable distance away from the object.

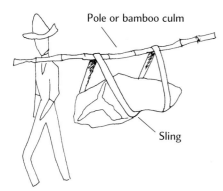

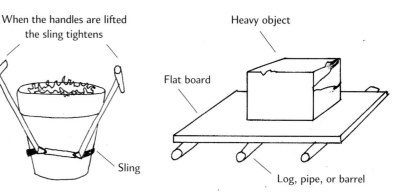

A pole sling can be used to distribute the weight of heavy objects and allow them to be lifted more easily. A pole of sweet chestnut or bamboo, combined with strapping, is all you need.

This pot lifter uses the same principle as the pole sling to enable two people to lift bulky objects up to 200 pounds. Another excellent way to lift heavy objects is to use a counterweight; modern cranes use this principle to lift heavy loads.

Linear roller bearings date back to the construction of the pyramids; the basic technique is still in use today. The simplest incarnation of this method is to use a line of tree trunks; as the heavy object is pulled, the logs roll along the ground, and as each log emerges from the back, it is returned to the front of the line.

Basic Principles of Sustainable Planting Design

As we have seen, the greener garden is all about trying to minimize the input required to create and maintain it. Every choice, from the bricks and stone used to create walls and paths to the compost used to prepare the soil, comes back to this simple principle. When we are planting the garden, the questions we need to ask ourselves are the same: How much energy was used to grow this plant? How much energy was used to transport it and to make the plant pots? How much attention will this plant require once it is in the ground? Will it require watering and fertilizer or will it thrive in the natural conditions of the site? Sustainable planting designs follow the lead of nature.

Matching Plant to Place

The most important principle in designing a sustainable planting scheme is to choose plants that will grow well in the natural conditions of the site. For centuries, gardeners have battled with their environment, adding lime to clay soil in an attempt to make it more alkaline, sinking acid-loving plants in giant pockets of ericaceous soil in an attempt to cheat nature. My grandparents spent hours and weeks lovingly watering their camellias with cold tea in an attempt to make them happy in the sandy soil of Surrey.

When you are trying to minimize the input needed to create and maintain a garden, there is no point fighting nature—trying to change the conditions of the garden to suit a fixed palette of plants. Sustainable planting is all about learning from nature, picking the right plant for the right place. However difficult a site may appear to be, nature provides the solution:

* In the exposed prairies of the United States, ornamental grasses such as switchgrass and moor grass thrive despite searing 80-mile-per-hour winds.

* In the dry shade of a woodland, deschampsia, foxglove, and euphorbia make a beautiful tapestry planting beneath a canopy of trees.

* In the cold, damp clay soils of the Midlands, willow thrives, providing sustainable fencing materials and charcoal.

* In a climate alternating between hot and dry, and cold and windy, lavender forms a useful crop in the Maritime Alps of southern France.

the United Kingdom, rosebay willowherb (*Epilobium angustifolium*) is no longer associated with overgrown railway tracks but with elegant naturalized planting for bees and butterflies, such as the white garden at Sticky Wicket in Dorset.

This is not to say that all native plants are garden worthy, or that all nonnative plants should be shunned. In the rush to promote the use of native plants in our gardens, something has been lost in translation. Let me remind you that non-native plants are not automatically the bad guys. Many non-native plants play an equally important role in supporting local biodiversity. *Rosa rugosa*, a native of east Asia, is a tough, wind-tolerant shrub with fat orange hips that provide an important food source for local birds. It is also tolerant of salt and drought, making it a useful plant for unpredictable weather conditions. The important thing is to choose plants that suit your local environment without dominating it.

The Biodiversity in Urban Gardens in Sheffield (BUGS) project undertook a survey of seventy urban gardens in Sheffield between 2001 and 2004. The gardens represented a range of sizes, types, and locations. This study could find no evidence that the proportion of native versus alien plants in a garden has any effect on the invertebrate wildlife it supports. The main factor affecting biodiversity of fauna was simply diversity of vegetation. In particular, the number of layers of vegetation (from bulbs to ground cover to shrubs and trees) was vital. In a world that is seeing increasing monoculture in our agriculture systems, your garden can be an important part of a wider mosaic of varied plants and high biodiversity, key to ensuring we maintain the web of life in years to come.

When choosing plants for your garden, you should assess each plant on its sustainability merits: its contribution to biodiversity; its ability to grow without additional food, water, or fuss; its tolerance of pests and diseases; its beauty and structure. Native plants can give us a head start in our decisions, as they are likely to be well adapted to the local region, but naturalized plants are equally important. Diversity of planting is key to the sustainable garden.

GREEN TIP Choose a number of natives and non-natives that suit your environment without dominating it, since diversity of planting is key to the sustainable garden. As a general rule, the more diverse the planting, the more wildlife will benefit.

Plant Communities

Plant communities are groups of plants that work together. We will look at companion planting and plant guilds later in the book, but for now we are going to look at some of the most common plant communities found in nature. How do woodland, prairie, and meadow habitats work? How does nature achieve that elusive balance of vigour, variety, succession, and scale? What can we learn about our own gardens by looking at nature?

Nature builds complex, dynamic habitats. Unlike traditional garden borders, where groups of plants are sufficiently ordered and segregated, drifts of planting duke it out with each other in dense overlapping layers. These tightly packed interlocking plantings act as a living mulch, preventing weeds from gaining a foothold. Increasing our planting density is one of the most important tips we can take from nature, as dense plantings require far less maintenance than plantings with conventional spacing.

Woodland

At one time woodland habitat dominated the surface of the earth. In fact all land would revert to woodland if we were to stop gardening. The main challenge posed by a woodland habitat is lack of light. Plants that flourish in woodland shade have three choices: emerge and retreat before the summer canopy cuts out the light (bulbs and corms such as cyclamen and bluebells); use wide or glossy leaves to extract maximum light (hosta or *Aucuba japonica*); or climb up into the canopy in search of sunshine (rambling roses). With a limited amount of sunshine available to them, plants in shady habitats spread slowly and form a dense tapestry.

At the woodland edge where there is more light available, plants are more boisterous. The evergreen wood spurge, *Euphorbia amygdaloides* var. *robbiae*, is particularly useful for a dry shady spot, but you will need to combine it with something equally aggressive, such as Solomon's seal, hellebore, or fringe cups, or it will take over the garden. Another feisty combination pairs *Brunnera* 'Jack Frost' with Japanese anemone for frothy spring "forget-me-not" flowers, large heart-shaped leaves, and autumn daisylike flowers. The aggressive nature of woodland edge plants will give you a more fluid planting scheme as factions battle for control, but there are plenty of vigorous plants to play with.

(top left) *Brunnera* 'Jack Frost' has beautiful heart-shaped leaves with silvery markings that really sing out of a shady planting.

(top right) *Euphorbia amygdaloides* var. *robbiae* (wood spurge) is another useful woodland plant, but it can be invasive, so partner it with something aggressive or it will take over.

(bottom left) The large, lush leaves that make hostas so desirable to gardeners probably evolved as a way of capturing the maximum amount of light in a shady spot.

(bottom right) The evergreen woodrush (*Luzula* spp.) makes an excellent foil for flowering bulbs and perennials.

GREEN TIP **Try a woodland plant combination where shade and drought prevail.**

Aim to have a third of your plants in bloom at any one time so that you can enjoy a succession of flowers like prairies offer.

Town gardens have a lot to learn from woodland habitats as they often suffer from similar conditions: shade from other buildings, drought from our overefficient guttering and drainage, even poor soil if lots of building rubble is buried in the garden. In this instance, a town garden would be the ultimate environment for a woodland planting combination to flourish—perhaps serviceberry (*Amelanchier canadensis*) underplanted with woodrush and spring flowering bulbs.

Prairie

Prairies are equally complex habitats that result from our first attempts to clear land for grazing and agriculture. An ever-changing combination of grasses, flowers, shrubs, and trees, prairies often move through a number of distinctive stages. Young prairies often emerge after land is cleared through burning; they contain a balance of flowering plants and grasses. As the prairie matures, the slower-growing (but more aggressive) grasses begin to dominate the scheme, leaving a minority of flowering perennials. Over the years, sub-shrubs and small trees sometimes jostle for a spot. At first glance the plants seem to be scattered about at random, but everywhere the plants are intermingling, there is a fight for survival going on as the land attempts to reforest itself.

We can learn a lot from prairies in our own approach to planting. First, we can note the importance of foliage as a foil to flowering plants, to balance a planting and help us take it all in without feeling overwhelmed by too much detail. In a mature prairie, grasses outnumber flowering perennials three to one, but in a garden we should aim for a more modest ratio—a balanced planting might be composed of a third flowering plants at any one moment. This way we can enjoy a succession of flowers, find our plantings easier to read, and create a relaxing and beautiful environment.

Another good lesson that prairies can teach us is that borders do not have to follow a traditional format—a series of increasingly tall perennials, shrubs, and climbers, viewed from one direction, with a wall or fence as the backdrop. Plantings are often best enjoyed from more than one direction—when they are backlit, when you look down on them from above, or when you look through a veil of wispy plants.

Meadow

Meadows are not a natural habitat either, but a result of traditional farming methods. Land would be cleared of trees and scrub so that a

(top left) A suprising number of the herbaceous plants we traditionally associate with the classic English garden border were actually introduced from the North American prairies.

(top right) Echinacea and monarda are commonly found in prairie-style plantings.

(bottom left) Wispy grasses such as *Molinia* species and *Stipa gigantea* are essential for plantings inspired by prairies.

(bottom right) Many of the later-flowering prairie plants, such as black-eyed Susan and goldenrod, are yellow.

GREEN TIP Allow areas of grass to grow long throughout spring and early summer in order to hide the unsightly dying foliage of spring bulbs.

grass crop could be grown to feed livestock in winter. The grass would be allowed to grow steadily through spring and early summer before a midsummer harvest; no grazing was allowed until after this summer harvest. This agricultural approach created a landscape with low fertility and a short growing season in which self-seeded wildflowers were able to keep up with aggressive grasses and regenerate year after year.

Sadly, the meadows that were once essential to agriculture have largely disappeared. As fertilizers were applied to increase productivity of the grass (and nitrogen levels increased), grasses began to outcompete wildflowers, even in the short growing season before harvest. The balance shifted, and traditional meadows were lost.

Meadows, or at least meadow-style plantings, are still very important in our romantic vision of nature, but they can also teach us some useful lessons about how to manage modern gardens. For gardeners struggling to improve the fertility and moisture-holding capacity of limestone soils, traditional meadows show us that there is another option. A beautiful range of wildflowers prefer an impoverished soil, so a palette of meadow cranesbill (*Geranium pratense*), camas lily (*Camassia leichtlinii*), and field scabiosa (*Knautia arvensis*) might be a better option.

The adoption of a midsummer cut can be just as useful in domestic gardens as it is in agricultural land. A trick many garden designers use is to create a meadowlike feel to a garden by allowing areas of grass to grow long throughout spring and early summer. The areas of longer grass tap into our romantic view of the past, but more important is that they hide the unsightly dying foliage of spring-flowering bulbs (which need several months to regenerate for a subsequent year's flowers). A midsummer cut will stop these areas of long grass from looking untidy. In the border, a midsummer cut of many perennials will give them a chance to regenerate and reflower.

Trees for Life

Trees are a part of any sustainable planting design, for they are essential to the health and equilibrium of the planet. They produce oxygen, filter and absorb pollutants, and provide food and shelter for birds, bugs, and animals, including humans. Historically, trees have played an essential role in human development, providing fuel, food, and building materi-

(top left) Camas lily is perfect for naturalizing in moist meadow plantings.

(top right) *Leucanthemum* species such as *L. vulgare* (ox-eye daisy) capture the quintessential look of a meadow but tend to be short-lived.

(bottom left) Meadow cranesbill is a useful meadow perennial that seeds about prolifically in long grass. This same quality can cause a problem when the plant is grown in a border.

(bottom right) Wildflowers in long grass create a romantic look.

GREEN TIP **Plant a shelterbelt of evergreen and deciduous trees to reduce heating bills in the winter and keep your house cooler in the summer.**

als. Modern materials have lessened our day-to-day reliance on trees, but they are still an important and treasured part of our environment.

Although all living plants absorb CO_2 as they photosynthesize, trees process carbon on such a grand scale that they have an essential role to play in the fight to control carbon emissions. The storage of CO_2 is known as carbon sequestration, and researchers are working hard to find the plants that sequester carbon most efficiently. Ultimately, trees of any shape, size, or species sequester carbon and thus are worth including in your garden. Where space allows, choose moderately fast-growing and long-lasting trees as they will sequester the most carbon.

David J. Nowak, a researcher at the U.S. Forest Service's Northern Research Station in Syracuse, New York, has studied the use of trees for carbon sequestration in urban settings across the United States. He recommends American sweetgum, bald cypress, black walnut, common horse-chestnut, Douglas fir, Hispaniolan pine, London plane, ponderosa pine, red oak, red pine, scarlet oak, Virginia live oak, and white pine as examples of trees especially good at absorbing and storing CO_2.

Trees play a pivotal role in the landscape, but they have the most powerful effect on a targeted, local scale. Trees are particularly important in urban areas, where they provide shade and help to improve the air quality and moderate the heat island effect. Trees protect us from the elements, filtering wind and rain, keeping us cool in summer and warm in winter. Fallen leaves enrich the soil while the overhead canopy and tangle of roots prevent soil erosion. Trees give shape and structure to the garden, screen unsightly views or frame a beautiful view, and absorb noise. Carefully chosen trees can even increase the value of your property.

When planning a garden, think about the long-term as well as immediate pleasure you will get from it. Trees can take anywhere from ten to two hundred years to mature from seed. Trees can be very long lived, with some ancient oaks living for six hundred years or more. You may be lucky enough to inherit some mature trees in your landscape, but all trees eventually come to the end of their life, so you mustn't forget to plan adequately for the long term, too—planting trees for future generations.

Most of us do not have enough room in our gardens for more than a couple of trees, so it can be a tricky decision to make. In small, urban gardens, you will need to limit your choices to small garden trees, or

The heat island effect describes how urban and built-up areas can develop a microclimate that makes them hotter than nearby rural areas. Roads and buildings can soak up huge amounts of heat during the day; the buildings prevent air from moving freely to offset the rise in temperature. Trees and other plants—in parks, foundation plantings, green roofs, and living walls—can help to moderate the temperature.

coppiced and pollarded specimens. In larger landscapes, you have more of a duty to include a variety of trees with different life spans so that the natural cycle of growth and decay is continued. If you have room for only one tree, it is best to plump for something that offers more than one season of interest. Look out for fruit, flowers, interesting bark, and autumn colour, and remember to check how big it will grow—you don't want to end up with a monster.

Choosing Plants from Sustainable Sources

Now that you've considered a planting scheme and thought about which trees to include, where are you going to get the plants? Keep in mind the key questions: How much energy was used to grow this plant? How much energy was used to transport it and to make the plant pots?

Production of trees can be energy intensive, especially if they are container grown abroad. The most sustainable choice is a field-grown specimen from a local nursery. Container-grown trees cannot access the water table or nutrients in the soil, so they require feeding and watering throughout the year. Even small container-grown whips can take more than five years to become carbon neutral. Field-grown trees are able to fend for themselves. They can be dug up for sale as a bare-root specimen in the dormant season and are a more sustainable choice.

The same thing can be said about production of plants: it can take a lot of energy, particularly if the plants are grown in containers far from the nursery where they're sold. Choosing plants that are locally grown is more sustainable; most sustainable is using plants you've grown yourself from seed, that have self-seeded, or that you've grown from cuttings. You can also increase the number of plants in your garden by dividing perennials that you already have.

Plants from seed

Growing plants from seed is a great way to reduce the costs (and the carbon footprint) of a garden. You can usually buy a whole packet of seeds for the cost of one plant, and they require far less energy to transport. That said, there are a number of excellent garden-worthy plants that take an interminably long time to mature from seed. Others are difficult to germinate without special equipment or require complex grafting, and these really are worth buying as mature plants.

GREEN TIP Include moderately fast-growing and long-lasting trees in your garden to sequester the most carbon.

Use plants you've grown yourself from cuttings or seed, or that have self-seeded. Increase the number of plants in your garden by dividing perennials.

The eight best trees for small gardens

- *Acer griseum*
- *Amelanchier lamarckii*
- *Corylus avellana 'Fuscorubra' (formerly 'Purpurea')*
- *Crataegus laevigata 'Paul's Scarlet'*
- *Malus tschonoskii*
- *Prunus ×subhirtella 'Autumnalis'*
- *Sambucus nigra*
- *Sorbus hupehensis*

Ten plants to grow from seed

- *Achillea* species
- *Agastache* species
- *Aquilegia* species
- *Atriplex hortensis* var. *rubra*
- *Digitalis* species
- *Echinacea* species
- *Foeniculum vulgare*
- *Nepeta* species
- *Rudbeckia* species
- *Trifolium rubens*
- *Verbena bonariensis*

Working out which plants you should grow from seed is not always easy and often requires a bit of knowledge. Some nursery catalogs rate their seeds according to difficulty, which can help. In general, fast-growing umbels (flat-topped composite flowerheads—a bit like an umbrella) such as yarrow, cow parsley, and fennel are easy to grow from seed. *Angelica gigas* (one of the giant umbellifers) is also very straightforward to grow from seed, and although it is a biennial (only flowering in its second year), the giant beetroot-red flowers are well worth waiting for.

Plants that seed themselves

When designing planting, I always like to include some nonsterile subjects (plants that seed themselves) to perpetuate my schemes. There is nothing more exciting than seeing your carefully planned planting scheme take on a life of its own, with plants weaving new layers as they set seed. Your borders will only improve as plants meander through the border, popping up where you least expect it.

For both formal and informal plantings, my current obsession is agastache—a short-lived midborder perennial that seeds itself well enough. The purple spires of *Agastache* 'Black Adder' associate brilliantly with the globe shapes of *Echinops ritro* 'Veitch's Blue' or *Eryngium yuccifolium* and giant mounds of phlox. Alternatively, pair agastache with brightly coloured echinacea, grand spires of phlomis, and one of the many ornamental grasses. For the front of the border you'll not go far wrong with pulmonaria, *Geranium pheum*, dianthus, and *Calamintha grandiflora*, which will happily seed themselves between other plants along the front edge without becoming a nuisance. For an informal gravel garden, *Stipa tenuissima* is an excellent choice. This feathery evergreen grass will dance around other self-perpetuating plants such as the stately *Eryngium giganteum* 'Miss Willmott's Ghost'.

You will need to exercise a degree of self-control when choosing nonsterile perennials. Some of the most prolific seeders can soon become pests if they are not kept in check. To halt the spread of aggressive perennials, such as lady's mantle and loosestrife, cut the spent flower heads off the plant before they set seed. Dominant perennials can vary from garden to garden. In a garden I was recently working on in Wales, baby knautia plants were springing up all over the place, but in my garden back in Nottingham, I have rarely seen a spare seedling. In many parts of the United States, monarda will soon threaten to outcompete its neighbours, and in part of Oxfordshire, *Centranthus ruber* grows out of every crevice.

Saving seed

For plants that do not reliably seed about on their own, and for seed swaps, it is worth taking the time to save some seed from your own plants. Many plants produce fantastic ornamental seed heads for wind pollination, and these are some of the easiest to collect. Keep an eye on your seed heads as they ripen, and when they look like they are just about to open, place a paper bag over the seed head, cut the stalk, and fold the bag over. After labeling your bag (otherwise it's so easy to muddle them up), pop it in a dry place for a few days. Once the seeds have been released, pick out any pieces of debris and funnel the seeds into paper envelopes. I like to label my seed envelopes with the plant name and date; then I pop them in a Tupperware box until it's time to sow them.

There is no point saving seed from hybrids, as they will not come true from seed and will not resemble the plant they came from. Hybrids usually have an × in the middle of their name, such as *Calamagrostis* ×*acutiflora* 'Karl Foerster' or *Salvia* ×*sylvestris* 'May Night'. Other plants that do not come true from seed include *Anthriscus sylvestris* 'Ravenswing', *Origanum* 'Herrenhausen', peonies, hostas, and most geraniums.

Plants from cuttings

It's easy to make more plants from your favourite shrub using cuttings—either for your own garden or for a neighbour. Cuttings are particularly useful for growing named cultivars, which don't come true from seed. Some of our favourite garden shrubs, trees, and woody perennials—including lavender, dogwoods, mock orange, and hydrangeas—can be propagated for free by taking cuttings.

Lots of different methods can be used to take cuttings, but the most common methods are softwood and hardwood cuttings. The type of cutting will depend upon the time of year and the plant you are propagating. Softwood cuttings are usually taken over the summer months when plants are producing plenty of firm, fresh shoots. As long as you can prevent them from wilting and drying out, they should establish new roots very quickly and will be ready to pot on in a couple of

Aggressive self-seeders

- *Acer saccharinum*
- *Alchemilla mollis*
- *Allium ursinum*
- *Anemone hupehensis* var. *japonica*
- *Buddleja* species
- *Campanula porscharskyana*
- *Convallaria majalis*
- *Euphorbia griffithii*
- *Geranium nodosum*
- *Gypsophilla paniculata*
- *Hesperis matronalis*
- *Lunaria* species; *L. rediva* is a less aggressive choice
- *Lythrum salicaria*
- *Myosotis sylvatica*
- *Persicaria bistorta*

PROJECT   Swap seeds

You can't sell seeds in the United Kingdom unless you have registered them on the National Seed List, and since this process costs £2000 per variety, many heritage and heirloom varieties are not on the list. In a bid to keep these "outlawed" varieties growing, seed swaps are springing up all over the place, allowing gardeners to swap these seeds through gardening clubs and websites. Garden Organic is building up a Heritage Seed Library (HSL) of heirloom varieties that are no longer widely available. Members of the Garden Organic HSL can apply for up to six rare varieties of vegetable seeds each year, and if they are really keen they can even volunteer as seed guardians. The Royal Horticultural Society (RHS) runs a similar seed distribution scheme for its members and sends out approximately 250,000 packets of seed each year.

In the United States, regulations make it difficult to import seeds from international seed swappers. Since 2002, the U.S. Department of Agriculture (USDA) has ruled that a phytosanitary certificate must accompany all parcels of seed imported into the United States. The paperwork puts most seed swappers off, and the RHS no longer sends seeds to members in the United States. Still, there are plenty of opportunities for gardeners to swap seeds within the United States, the foremost of which is the Seed Savers Exchange in Iowa, which has been saving and sharing heirloom seeds with its members since 1975.

GREEN TIP **Try planting your hardwood cuttings of dogwood, willow, and butterfly bush directly outside in a sheltered part of the garden. Place them in a narrow, well-drained trench with a layer of sand at the base.**

months. Hardwood cuttings are taken in the dormant season, once all the leaves have fallen off the trees. They are easy and reliable, so are an ideal way to start learning about cuttings, but they can be slow to grow and will usually not begin to root until the following spring.

Dividing perennials

Most perennials benefit from division every three to five years to maintain flowering vigour and health, but this technique can also be used to control the size of rapidly growing plants, as well as to create lots of new plants—for free! Plants can be successfully divided at almost any time of year (as long as they are kept well watered); however, your plants will be happiest if you divide them when the plant is dormant. By dividing summer-flowering plants in spring or autumn, and spring-flowering plants in summer, you will give yourself the best chance of success.

I prefer to wait until autumn before I divide any of my plants. At this time of year, many of my favourite perennials are beginning to die

Taking a softwood cutting

1. Cut a healthy firm shoot from the plant (lateral shoots are best). The best way to learn if a stem is ready for softwood cuttings is to bend it. If it snaps, it's ready to be cut. Avoid any shoots with evidence of flowers.

2. Trim your cutting to 8 to 13 cm (3 to 5 in) long by making a straight cut beneath a pair of leaves; then remove the lower sets of leaves. Keep only one or two pairs of leaves at the top of your cutting.

3. Dip each cutting in a rooting hormone.

4. Push your cutting into a pot of free-draining cutting compost so that only the leaves are visible and water well. You can pot up several cuttings in each container as long as you leave at least 5 cm (2 in) between cuttings.

5. Put in a propagator or cover the pot with a clear plastic bag (held in place with an elastic band). Keep your cuttings damp and in a light place while they form new roots.

6. After about three weeks, give your cuttings a little tug to see if they have rooted. Pot each rooted cutting individually and then plant out when they have filled their new pot with roots.

Taking a hardwood cutting

1. Cut a healthy piece of woody growth from the plant, about the thickness of a pencil, before removing any soft new growth at the tip. Avoid any stems that have been damaged by pests or disease.

2. Divide this stem into sections approximately 15 to 30 cm (6 to 12 in) long, making a clean sloping cut above a bud at the top of each section and a straight cut across at the base.

3. Dip each cutting in a rooting hormone.

4. Push your cutting into a pot of free-draining cutting compost so that only the top buds are visible and water well.

5. You can pot up several cuttings in each container as long as you leave at least 5 cm (2 in) between cuttings. By autumn, your cuttings should be well rooted and can be hardened off and planted out into the garden.

PROJECT   Increase the number of plants through division

Once you have identified the plant you intend to divide, give it a quick tidy-up with some pruning shears, removing any dead leaves and stems. At the same time, it is often worth pruning the foliage back firmly to lessen any stress from leaf evaporation once the divisions have been replanted. Using a hand fork, gently loosen the soil around the plant so that you will be able to lift it without damaging the essential root system. Give it a shake to get rid of the loose soil.

Fibrous-rooted plants such as coral bells and prim-rose, which have only a loose tangle of roots, can usu-ally be pulled apart by hand without damaging the plants. For more firmly knotted roots, on plants such as day lilies, you may need the help of a couple of hand forks to lever the sections apart. Discard any old, woody growth from the centre of the plant and replant before the roots dry out. Keep your newly divided plants well watered while they establish.

Plants with fleshy roots or woody crowns will require a little more force. This group includes peony and Japanese anemone. Cut the plant into sections using a sharp spade. Iris corms respond particularly well to division in this way.

You can separate one plant into a number of new plants, as long as each section has at least one healthy bud and a decent number of roots. Most plants divide easily into three or five sections.

Some plants, such as ajuga and liriope, spread by stolons to produce little plantlets. Just as you would with an indoor spider plant, you can simply detach and replant these baby plants.

These two hand forks are inserted back-to-back in the middle of the plant; gently pushing the handles back and forth will cause the prongs to gradually tease the plant apart.

back or can be pruned back so that I can see what is going on in the border I am tackling. The efficient (some say lazy) gardener in me is also appeased, as I can expect reliable levels of autumn rainfall to take care of my newly divided plants for me.

7

Preparing Soil and Planting

By now you should have a clear idea of the hard landscaping materials you want to use in your greener garden, as well as the kinds of plants you want to grow in order to cooperate with the conditions in your yard. It's finally time to think about planting. Planting a garden that will withstand storms and/or drought, whatever the changing climate dishes out, conserves resources by protecting your investment of time and materials. It begins with preparing the soil.

Bed preparation is not a glamorous job, but time spent eradicating perennial weeds and improving your soil will reap great rewards. Creating good soil is hard work and can appear to be very time consuming, but I reckon that for every hour you spend on soil preparation, you will be saving five hours dealing with weeds, pests, disease, and irrigation concerns. Good soil preparation, plus knowing when and how to plant, will reward you with a garden that is quick to establish and tough enough to stand up against unpredictable weather.

The Importance of Preparing Your Beds

Thorough soil preparation is the key to the storm- and drought-tolerant garden. Plants growing in well-structured, well-drained soil will be able to cope with almost anything. They will develop strong root systems that will tap into supplies of water, oxygen, and nutrients deep underground, giving them the ability to cope with the stress of storms and drought and to fight off pests and diseases.

It's amazing which plant rules you will be able to break if you get your soil preparation right. When I first put a spade in my garden soil, it came out with a square hunk of clay. A few years of soil building later, I am rewarded with mixed herbaceous borders in which even clay-hating plants such as Russian sage thrive.

It can be very tempting to skip over the job of preparing your soil in favor of the more exciting job of choosing and installing the plants, but this is always a mistake and will cause you problems farther down the line. Think about soil as the foundation of a garden. You wouldn't leave out the foundations of a house, would you? If you are a garden designer or landscaper, you may need to educate your clients about the importance of investing in proper soil preparation. If you are a garden owner, make sure you check the soil preparation before you allow contractors to move on to the planting of a new garden.

Eliminating Perennial Weeds

Before you even think about improving the structure of your soil, you will need to tackle any pernicious weeds. Don't put this job off, thinking you will deal with the weeds as you go along—some of these boys are nasty and will be almost impossible to get rid of once your garden has been planted. The good news is that if you can get rid of the most aggressive perennial weeds before you plant your garden, you will have reduced the future maintenance by half.

Perennial weeds, such as ground elder, bindweed, and thistles, can be hard to kill because of their vigorous, spreading root system. This root system anchors them deep underground and will often snap off when you attempt to remove the weeds by pulling or digging. The majority of perennial weeds are able to regenerate from very small pieces of root (or more accurately, from underground sections of rhizome), so trying to eradicate them can be frustrating.

Smothering

One of the best ways to eliminate perennial weeds is to smother them, but it takes a very patient gardener to succeed with this approach. The theory is that if you exclude the light plants require to photosynthesize and make food, they will weaken and eventually die. Unfortunately, perennial weeds are fighters and it can be years before they finally give up the ghost.

Although light exclusion, or smothering, is not the quickest process, it will be the most efficient use of your time and energy—and can save you an awful lot of digging later on. Several layers of dampened cardboard or newspaper, or thick black plastic sheeting, are the most popular choices, but you can use any scrap material that will successfully exclude light, such as old shower curtains or old carpet. For the best results, you will have to keep those weeds in the dark for six months to two years.

Digging and chemicals

Some perennial weeds respond so slowly to light exclusion that you will want to resort to a good old-fashioned spade. For perennial weeds with shallow spreading roots, such as ground elder, this can provide an effective control—providing no sections of root are left in the soil

GREEN TIP To reduce future maintenance by half, tackle weeds before you plant. Smother them or dig them out; use chemicals only as a last resort and be sure to follow the instructions on the package.

Research has shown that about 80 percent of all plant problems are related to poor soil.

GREEN TIP In autumn, leave stubborn clods of clay soil on the surface of the bed so that the winter frost will help to break them down. Just remember not to dig (or walk on) the soil when it is wet or you will undo all your hard work. You can dig light, sandy soils year-round.

to regenerate. For deep-rooting plants, such as Japanese knotweed and bindweed, digging is never really going to be a permanent solution, as their roots can penetrate several metres down and will regrow from even the smallest fragment. To make the job of digging out the rhizomes a bit easier, many gardeners choose to repeatedly cut down the foliage first in an attempt to weaken the plant.

Although chemicals should not be the first port of call for any gardener, there are times when the use of chemicals is the only sensible option. For example, there is no quick fix when it comes to Japanese knotweed; even with a systemic weed killer, it will take about three years to eradicate this perennial weed. In the rare instance where you decide chemicals really are the most sensible solution, make sure you apply them at the right stage of the weed's life cycle following the instructions on the container.

Improving Your Soil

There is an argument that soils do not need to be improved, plant choices do. There are plants to cope with any situation, especially when it comes to thin or low-nutrient soils. Some of the most beautiful wildflower meadows require a thin, depleted soil, while other plants grow best in aggregate without any soil at all.

While I agree that it can be dangerous to add too many nutrients to the soil, I am always in favour of improving the soil structure. Any type of soil can be improved with the right treatment, so don't worry too much about what you've got. Organic matter is the key to great soil, and everything from compost to leaf mould and bark chippings—even shredded clothing—will help to turn your basic soil type into a dark, moist, crumbly soil. In most cases, you will get the best results from laying your organic material on top of the soil as a topdressing or mulch. If you are determined to fork it through the border, make sure the soil is dry so that you do not damage the existing soil structure—you can do more harm than good if you are not careful.

If you are preparing a new bed for planting, try to add a good 10 to 15 cm (4 to 6 in) of organic matter to the soil. A lot of the mulch will get mixed in with the existing soil when you come to plant, and the rest will be slowly incorporated into the soil by worms. If you are mulching an established border, a shallow 5 cm (2 in) mulch should do the trick in late autumn and/or early spring. Growing green manures can also help.

If you have acres of brambles to clear, you might want to consider borrowing some Highland cattle. They will eat pretty much anything and are well known for their ability to clear brush, broom, and brambles.

Homemade compost

Compost is probably the most valuable soil additive. It improves the structure of both sandy and clay soil, helping sandy soil hold water and nutrients and helping clay soil release them. As a general rule, dry sandy soils benefit the most from rich, moist organic matter, while wet clay soils respond best to dry, fibrous material, but all organic matter will eventually improve your soil if you keep adding it at least twice a year.

This is your chance to use the lovely compost you learned how to prepare in chapter 2. A 5-cm (2-in) layer of compost on the surface of the soil is ideal. For hungry vegetable borders, you might want to add closer to 10 cm (4 in).

Composting materials from your own garden makes the most sense, keeping the risk of introducing contaminated materials into your garden's ecosystem to a minimum.

GREEN TIP **Add organic matter to the surface of your soil at least twice a year, in fall and spring, to improve soil and plant health. A 5-cm (2-in) layer will do the trick for established borders and beds.**

Clay mixed well into sandy soil can help to improve the structure of the soil—but not the other way around.

Sand

Sand improves drainage but only in massive quantities. Small amounts of sand in clay soil can bind soil tighter, making the problem worse, so adding sand is a technique best avoided unless you are trying to manufacture tonnes and tonnes of soil. For sand to have a positive effect on the drainage of clay soil, you would need to add at least one-third sand, so compost is a better choice.

Grit and other aggregates

Coarse aggregates such as grit, perlite, and gravel can be added to clay soil to improve its structure. These aggregates are usually not very effective on their own, but this can be a useful way to recycle materials on-site and can work well in combination with organic materials such as compost or mineralized straw.

Mushroom compost

A by-product from mushroom production, mushroom compost is one of the best ways to give structure to a heavy clay soil. It is light to fork onto the surface, but you may get one or two mushrooms growing in the first year. You should be able to find a local mushroom farm simply by looking in the telephone directory. Most mushroom farms are only too happy to sell their spent mushroom compost (which is waste material for them) for a pittance. Mushroom compost is slightly alkaline, so it should not be applied too regularly for fear of raising the pH too much.

Organic gardeners will need to be careful when sourcing mushroom compost as it may contain pesticide residues, particularly organochlorides used against the fungus gnat, if it is not from an organic mushroom farm.

Mineralized straw

A mineralized straw, such as the British product known as Strulch, is a good alternative to mushroom compost (and arguably an improvement over it). It has a neutral pH and is light and easy to handle but does not blow around the garden. Strulch lasts about three times as long as untreated straw, so it can be left on the ground for up to two years. Certified organic by the Soil Association, it can also be worked into the soil at the end of the season to improve soil structure and drainage. Popular with estates and gardeners across the United Kingdom, it's currently being used at the Eden Project and the Royal Horticultural Society gardens at Wisley and should become available in the United States and Canada.

Composted bark

Another coarse material that can be used to add much needed structure to clay soil is composted bark chippings. Low in nutrients, this light, bulky material will help to loosen heavy clay soil—but make sure the chips have been composted, or they will rob the soil of nitrogen as they decompose. If you are clearing any trees or shrubs from the site, remember to keep this material on-site. It can be useful for making wildlife habitats or composting into a soil conditioner or mulch.

Leaf mould

Leaf mould (which you learned how to make in chapter 2) is truly wonderful stuff. It is great for soil improvement, makes a brilliant mulch, and is the secret ingredient in many seed and potting mixes. When you are sweeping up your garden leaves, remember to use only the deciduous leaves to make leaf mould, as evergreen leaves will not break down properly. Leaves vary in acidity, so try to get a good mix for a neutral pH compost.

Wood ash

Wood ash can be used to raise the pH of acid soil. It is particularly useful in the acid soils of the southern and eastern United States but can increase existing pH and/or salt problems in western soils.

Gypsum

Traditionally, gypsum (calcium sulphate) is applied to clay soils that have been flooded by the sea. As well as helping to mitigate the effects of sea salt, gypsum can also help to improve the structure of some clay soils that are lacking in calcium.

Peat moss and coir

It is widely accepted that peat moss is unsustainable and should not be used by gardeners. Peat bogs are a type of wetland that is thought to cover approximately 3 percent of the earth. The largest peat bogs are found in Finland, followed by Canada, Ireland, and Sweden. Some scientists believe that peat bogs are as important as the rain forests and just as fragile. There is concern that global peat extraction is irrevocably destroying wildlife habitats and releasing CO_2. The Royal Horticultural Society advises gardeners that it considers the purchase of peat to be "unacceptable for the primary use of soil incorporation and ground mulching."

On the other hand, peat can be a renewable resource. Canadian peat bogs cover such a wide area that the peat is growing nearly sixty times as fast as it is being harvested. In Canada, a single bog is harvested for between fifteen and sixty years before it is returned to wetland. Stringent controls mean that at least 1 m (3.3. ft) of peat is left at the bottom of any bog that is commercially harvested, which helps it regrow.

Peat bogs play an important role in sequestering carbon. Peat dug up in Britain for garden compost releases almost half a million tonnes of carbon dioxide a year—the equivalent of 100,000 cars on the road.

Harvested peat lands can be restored to ecologically balanced systems within five to twenty years after peat harvesting.

Whether peat bog restoration is possible is a matter of heated debate. There is a concern that the ecosystem is so delicately balanced that these managed bogs are still putting species at risk. Whichever way you argue it, transport miles may rule out the use of Canadian peat moss for gardeners in the United Kingdom and large parts of the United States. Consumers wanting to buy peat from a bog where strict environmental guidelines are in place should look out for the Canadian Sphagnum Peat Moss Association (CSPMA) logo.

Coir is commonly suggested as a peat substitute. It provides drainage but few nutrients. Although coir is sustainably produced, it tends to originate in the tropics and can rack up huge transport miles before it reaches your garden. If the coir you find for sale is not produced locally, leaf mould or compost may be a better choice.

Topsoil

Many people, even some gardening professionals, think that the only thing you need to do to prepare a garden for planting is to buy in some topsoil and dump it on the garden. Nothing could be further from the truth. Topsoil is usually of unknown origin. There are no trade standards regulating topsoil. It may contain near-inert subsoil, weed seeds, chemical or pesticide residue, or depleted agricultural soil and is likely to do very little to improve the soil structure or water-holding capacity. Avoid buying in topsoil. It is a waste of money, and almost any of the other choices for improving your soil will be better.

If topsoil is stripped from your site during construction, it is better to store the soil for reuse on the site than to pay someone to cart it away and then later buy topsoil back in when it is time to plant the garden. Topsoil should be stored in shallow piles and covered with breathable material. This slows drying, limits dust, excludes windblown seeds, and avoids mud, sedimentation, and erosion. The maximum recommended depth of piled soil varies between 1.8 m (6 ft) for sandy soil and 1.2 m (4 ft) for clay soil.

Soil is a living material full of microorganisms, so it is best to store topsoil for as short a time as possible. Short storage times are often impractical, but if you know you will need to store your soil for lon-

GREEN TIP When removing turf to create a planting area (perhaps widening a border), don't put the stripped turf in the skip. Instead turn it over and leave it at the bottom of the new planting bed where it will rot down to make lovely new topsoil. This will keep the worms and microorganisms just where you want them, maintaining soil health.

GREEN TIP Add alginic acid to soil in pots in order to increase its water-holding capacity. In the United States, look for Grandma Enggy's Seaweed Extract (www. advancednutrients.com/tech_info/ seaweed_extract_tech_info. html). U.K. gardeners can look for Natural Gardening Complete Soak (www.naturalgardening.co.uk/ complete_soak.phtml).

ger, you can mediate the effects on soil health with a few simple tricks. Water the soil so that it remains moderately damp and consider growing a quick crop of green manure to stabilize the pile.

Water-retaining granules

Most successful water-retaining granules are based on synthetic polymers, which can absorb and release moisture over an extended period. Best known for reducing the watering requirements of hanging baskets and containers, these water-retaining polymers can increase the soil's water-holding capacity by as much as 1000 percent. Some can even absorb soluble nutrients and prevent leaching of water and nutrients in poor soils.

A far more sustainable choice is to use a natural material with the same water-holding qualities. Shredded clothing has been a favourite soil additive with allotment holders for many years, but it does little to improve the water-holding capacity of the soil. Alginic acid, a natural water-storing gel made from brown algae, at last offers a real alternative to synthetic polymers. It has been used for years in the pharmaceutical industry and for thickening soups and jellies. In the United Kingdom, it is available to the home gardener as Natural Gardening Complete Soak and in the United States as Grandma Enggy's Seaweed Extract.

Green manures—grow your own soil conditioner

Green manures are often overlooked when it comes to improving the structure of your soil. They can be an inexpensive way to prepare new land for use. Lupines, fodder radish, and alfalfa all use fibrous taproots to break up the subsoil, while forming a ground cover that prevents soil erosion and prevents weeds from colonizing. Green manures have traditionally been used to restore arable land, adding bulk and nutrients to the soil, but they are equally useful in domestic gardens.

These green manures work in two main ways, fixing nitrogen and providing food for composters in the soil. Legumes are popular for their ability to fix nitrogen: nodules on their roots contain bacteria that can take nitrogen from the air for the plant to use in growth. Once the green manure has been dug into the soil, this nitrogen becomes available for future plantings. Non-legume plantings do not have the ability to fix nitrogen, but they often produce more organic matter. They have a better root system, so they tend to be a better choice for extreme weather conditions and poor soils.

(top left) Clover makes an excellent living mulch or long-term green manure.

(top right) Alfalfa is one of the best green manures for dry soil; its deep taproots help to improve the soil structure and also fix nitrogen in the soil.

(bottom left) Comfrey is an excellent plant to grow as the leaves can be used to make a lovely, nutritious plant feed. But don't be tempted to use it as a green manure as it can be very hard to get rid of once established.

(bottom right) Phacelia is a quick growing groundcover that smothers weeds and improves soil structure. Tolerant of most soil types, it is particularly useful in dry soils

GREEN TIP **Chop up your green manure while the stems are still soft and dig it into the soil to a depth of about 15 cm (6 in). The soft bruised stems will quickly break down, so the border can be planted after only a couple of weeks.**

If you are using a green manure to prepare beds in your vegetable garden, remember to follow the rules of crop rotation. Don't use a legume such as field beans for your green manure if you are planning to grow runner beans or garden peas in the soil afterward.

Although many green manures can be sown all year, autumn is the best time to sow them. Vegetable plots are generally empty, and people are spending less time in their gardens over the winter months. A green manure will suppress weeds, fix nitrogen, and may even help to break up the subsoil.

Here are some good green manures to consider:

ALFALFA. Alfalfa is an excellent green manure for dry soil and is sometimes described as a complete natural fertilizer. Its deep roots improve the structure of the subsoil while also fixing nitrogen. Sow from midspring to midsummer. Turn into the soil in the autumn or leave to stand throughout the winter.

CRIMSON CLOVER. Clovers are a popular choice for green manures. Crimson clover is a quick-growing clover that makes an excellent weed suppressant. It is not normally winter hardy as it dislikes waterlogged and heavy soils, but you may have luck overwintering this clover in a sandy soil.

FIELD BEANS. A hardy nitrogen-fixing green manure for clay soil, field beans can be sown as late as late autumn and are a good choice for overwintering.

FODDER RADISH. With its deep taproot, fodder radish will reliably improve the subsoil. Fodder radish produces plenty of organic matter. It gradually dies down over the winter, making it easy to incorporate into the soil in spring.

HUNGARIAN GRAZING RYE. One of the best overwintering green manures for clay soil, Hungarian grazing rye will prevent soil erosion and nutrient leaching. Sow in late summer or early autumn and dig back into the soil in spring.

TARES. Although it hates acid soil, tares can be another good overwintering choice for a nitrogen-fixing green manure.

WHITE CLOVER. White clover forms a low-growing ground cover that is also ideal for intercropping between rows of vegetables. Use this nitrogen-fixing clover as a living mulch or long-term green manure.

Fertilizer

Getting your soil structure right is hugely important, but you should be wary of overfeeding your soil. After all, plants respond well to adversity. They flower when they feel threatened so that they can be sure of their family line. A mollycoddled plant will produce wonderful lush foliage but may feel too comfortable to flower well. Lots of gardeners will disagree with me on this point, and reams of text have been written on nutritional additives for soil, but I believe if you improve your soil structure and mulch with organic material, your plants will get plenty of nutrition.

Manufacturing Soil

Even in a landscape that seems to have little soil available, it is possible to recycle discarded materials to create a growing medium that allows us to regenerate landscapes. In *Urban Soil in Landscape Design*, Phillip J. Craul wrote: "In most cities, you have got all the components you need for making soil—and it's all recycled." Soil is simply a mix of chemical, mineral, and organic components—so in the same way that gardeners create their own potting mix using compost and vermiculite, soil can be manufactured locally from a mixture of recycled materials. Recycled ground glass, sand from river dredgings, even washings from aggregate plants can be mixed with composted organic material to create soil.

Brick rubble can easily be amended as planting medium, especially if it has been on-site for years. Brick started its life as clay, which is a component of soil, so there is plenty of phosphorous, potassium, and magnesium available. The main problem with brick rubble is that it contains only low levels of nitrogen, but this can be solved by growing nitrogen-fixing plants, such as clover or tares. Once the rubble has been allowed to break down, the resulting soil tends to have excellent texture, drainage, and aeration.

Other types of rubble are trickier. Concrete rubble breaks down more slowly than brick rubble and contains fewer nutrients, so it would be better treated like a gravel garden to grow the sorts of plants that thrive on a depleted soil.

GREEN TIP Be careful not to add too much fertility to the soil as too much nitrogen encourages weeds. Avoid high carbon-to-nitrogen choices such as horse manure, straw, and wood chips, unless your soil is very high in nitrogen. Compost that is not fully mature can steal nitrogen from the soil, depriving plants.

PROJECT   To dig or not to dig?

Although it is often worth digging or double digging a border when you first create a new area of the garden, digging (and particularly rotovating or rototilling) can often do more harm than good. Digging can be very damaging to the soil structure. It can dry out the soil, destroy worm burrows, and introduce too much oxygen to the soil. Clay soil is especially vulnerable and is easily compacted when gardeners stand or walk on their beds.

Worms are important for healthy soil. Tunneling worms improve soil aeration and soil structure. They help water to infiltrate into the soil and they distribute organic matter and nutrients throughout the soil. The tunnels worms make as they move through the soil allow plant roots to delve more deeply into the subsoil where moisture can reliably be found—even in times of drought. Amazingly, worms can get through half their own weight in organic matter every day, recycling the bits they don't need back into the soil as worm casts. These worm casts are high in nitrogen, phosphorous, and potassium, all essential nutrients for healthy plant growth.

Research carried out by Wade H. Elmer at the Connecticut Agricultural Experiment Station demonstrates that earthworms also play a significant role in suppressing common soil-borne plant pathogens. A greenhouse study was carried out with asparagus, aubergines (eggplant), and tomatoes grown in pots infected with common *Fusarium* and *Verticillium* species known to cause serious plant diseases in these crops. In the pots that also contained earthworms, plant weights increased 60 percent, and estimates of disease severity declined 50 to 70 percent.

It is far better to layer organic nutrients on the surface of your bed and allow the worms to do the work than it is to dig over the border and risk cutting worms in half and damaging their ecosystem. Healthy soil contains lots of worm tunnels and air pockets. These provide oxygen for the community of worms, arthropods, and microorganisms that call soil home. Compacted soil has very few air pockets and is prone to flooding as the water struggles to infiltrate the soil.

Worms are not the only creatures that will benefit from a no-dig system. Spiders, beetles, and microorganisms such as nematodes all work together in a healthy soil, and they all need air and water to survive. The best way to build up a thriving soil community is to avoid walking on or digging through your beds. Make sure you provide plenty of organic matter by adding compost or leaf mould to the surface, and ensure your soil stays moist by mulching and planting closely to prevent soil erosion and evaporation.

Double digging cultivates soil to the depth of two spades. You have to be careful not to mix the two layers (subsoil and topsoil) when you are creating your trenches.

Planting—When and How

The planting season traditionally falls in the autumn. At this time of year, the temperatures have dropped but the soil should still be warm enough to plant, nurseries often have the best selection of perennial plants, and there is the promise of reliable rainfall throughout autumn and winter. But in areas with early autumn frosts, or where the soil is particularly cold and wet over the winter, spring can be a better time to establish new plants. Even small perennials planted in spring can easily mature in time for summer.

The idea when planting a new garden is to take advantage of the natural seasons so that you give your plants the best possible start with the least amount of fuss. Planting in the autumn will give plants plenty of time to develop a strong underground root system before top growth races away in the spring. Planting in the spring does not give plants as long to develop their roots, but it does mean that plants are not exposed to the ravages of the winter climate. Some gardeners choose to plant their hardy trees and shrubs in the autumn and fill in the gaps with more tender perennials in the spring. In the United Kingdom, it is nearly always best to plant in the autumn, but in the United States, planting times vary much more in different parts of the country.

For larger trees and shrubs, and for hedging, the best time to plant is in the dormant season—over the winter months. At this time of year, even large specimens can be moved without too much distress. The bare-root season runs between late autumn and early spring each year and is worth waiting for, as bare-root specimens can cost significantly less than containerized plants.

Moving or transplanting

Most people don't realize how delicate the root systems of their plants are—that's why we are tempted to break the rules and move plants in the heat of summer. We know that in theory we should wait for the dormant season, but it can be so frustrating to want to move that shrub in the midst of summer when we can see how well it would go with our rambling rose. The truth is that the root systems of even the smallest plants are huge. Roots systems are so extensive that there is usually as much root growth under the ground as there is leafy growth above the ground.

GREEN TIP When you plant a new garden, time it to take advantage of the seasons so your plants get the best possible start with the least amount of fuss. Plant larger trees and shrubs—and move established specimens—in the dormant season.

An eight-year-old tall tree with branches 10 feet wide may have a root system up to 30 feet across. Until the roots have regrown, plants that are moved may not put on any new growth above the ground. When larger shrubs and trees are transplanted, the required root growth is so extensive the plant is often described as going into shock.

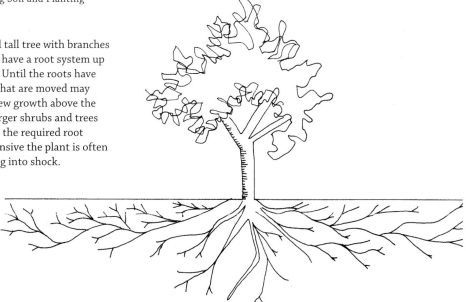

GREEN TIP **Always buy your roses bare root. Although roses can be bought as container-grown specimens throughout the year, you can also buy them bare root between late autumn and early spring. Bare-root specimens are quick to establish and are much cheaper than container-grown roses—especially if you are buying them mail order, as they are much lighter to post.**

When a plant is dug up, more than three-quarters of the root system can be lost in an instant. This is an enormous shock. Add to that the stresses of spring growth, the energy demands of flowering, and the heat of the summer sunshine and you can see why moving a plant in summer might well cause it to throw a tantrum.

When transplanting shrubs and perennials, we often assume that the root system extends only as far as we can see the root growing - overlooking the microscopic root hairs at the outer reaches. In fact, over half of a plant's root system is invisible to the naked eye. A good rule of thumb is that the root system of a plant usually extends to at least the edge of the canopy.

To limit the trauma of transplanting specimens, try to move plants only in the dormant season. Light drizzle is ideal. Tiny root hairs can dry out very quickly, even in cool weather, so the quicker you can replant, the better. Water newly planted trees and shrubs well to encourage strong new roots to grow.

Bulbs

Bulbs are traditionally planted between early and late autumn but you often have to order your bulbs as early as midsummer to ensure you get the most popular varieties. In clay soil, or in soil that is heavy and wet over winter, it is best to get your bulbs planted as early as possible so that the roots can start growing immediately. You can get away with planting your bulbs in pots as late as midwinter in some cases, but it's a bit of a gamble. The exception to the rule are snowdrops, which establish better when planted "in the green" in spring.

Plant sizes

Planted at the right time of year in well-prepared soil, plants will establish unbelievably quickly. Garden owners are consistently amazed at how quickly tiny 9-cm (4-in) plants knit together to form an established-looking border. In fact, most perennials do best if planted at 9 cm (4 in). They will have developed a strong enough root system to cope with the move into soil but will be less likely to go into shock than a larger plant and will grow more rapidly.

Frustratingly, very few retail nurseries offer plants for sale at 9 cm (4 in). Most retail nurseries offer plants for sale at 2 litres in the United Kingdom and 1 gallon in the United States, as they rely largely on impulse buys and have to provide specimens with enough flowers and growth to tempt us into a quick sale. It is worth making the effort to search out 9-cm (4-in) specimens (or asking a garden designer to get hold of the plants for you) because they will cost half the price, be easier to plant, and produce a quicker, healthier result.

How to plant

It is important to lay out your plants before you begin planting. You will find that even the most precise plan needs tweaking, and this is easy to do by simply swapping some of the plants around until you are happy with the composition. In the same way as I do when first constructing a planting plan, I place the structural plants (such as sedums and euphorbia) first. These anchor the scheme and make it easier to fill in the rhythm of the planting with drifts and the occasional flourish. Only once all the main herbaceous plants have been planted do I overlay the bulbs and filler plants.

With good soil preparation and small 9-cm plants, planting is the easy bit. Simply ease the plant out of the pot, split the roots a bit, and plant it at the same depth as it was growing in the pot. If you come across a plant that is beginning to get root-bound and where the roots are too tough to rip with your bare hands, you can use a pair of pruning shears to make a few snips to break up the root-ball.

GREEN TIP **If you can obtain them, plant 9-cm (4-in) perennials rather than larger specimens. If you can't get hold of 9-cm (4-in) plants, you can sometimes split a 2-L (1-gal) plant into several smaller pieces.**

If a 9-cm (4-in) perennial and a 2-L (1-gal) perennial are planted side by side in spring, by early summer the 9-cm plant will have overtaken the 2-L plant in both size and vigour.

Make sure your plants are all well watered before planting, or the surrounding soil will suck all the moisture out of the plant and cause it to wilt.

(right) When planting irises, remember to leave the fleshy corm exposed on top of the soil. *Iris germanica* needs sunlight to ripen their corms and can rot if buried under the soil.

I like to use a small hand trowel to plant. In well-prepared soil, you can lever the soil to one side with your hand trowel, slide in the plant, and then remove the trowel so that the soil slips back down to fill the gaps. After firming the soil down around the plant roots, you are ready for the next one. In this way, you can easily plant a couple of hundred 9-cm (4-in) pots in an hour.

Mound planting

Mound planting can be a useful way to reduce root rot when planting in heavy, poorly drained soils. Although this traditional technique has been around for centuries, it has become a rare sight in twenty-first-century gardens. Mound planting can be used to prevent "wet feet" especially among fruit trees such as apples, cherries, and berries. For the best chance of success, you will need to create a mound at least 30 cm (1 ft) high and five times the width of the root-ball. Mix plenty of grit and compost into your heavy soil so that your new mound is free draining, then firm it by treading it down lightly with the heel of your foot before planting.

Watering new plantings

Planting your garden at the right time of year should remove most of the demands for supplementary watering. It is always worth giving your plants a good soaking immediately after planting. Watering at the base of the plant, you should water until the soil is saturated (and water is running off the surface), then allow the water to drain into the soil for ten to thirty minutes and repeat. Once plants are established in the garden, they should require very little supplemental watering. If you have prepared your soil well and chosen the right plants, you will be able to avoid extra watering altogether.

8

Selecting Plants for
Challenging Conditions

Gardens across the world are afflicted by a wide range of weather damage through the course of the year, from storms and hurricanes to drought. But each garden usually has one primary challenge that needs to be addressed first and foremost. You know what yours is. The good news is that plants exist that will do well in any condition that nature might dish out. This chapter gives you suggestions to consider as you assemble your plant list.

Plants That Tolerate Drought

All plants rely on water to stay alive. They use energy from the sun to split water into its two elements, hydrogen and oxygen. The hydrogen combines with carbon dioxide in the air to produce the sugars that nourish the plant, and the excess oxygen is released into the atmosphere. Plants also need oxygen to convert that food to energy (just like we do). In hot weather, plants also use water to keep themselves cool, by allowing water to evaporate through thousands of stomata on the undersides of their leaves.

Most plants get their water from the ground, so a good root system is important for any plant hoping to cope with drought. A deep taproot goes straight down into the ground, tapping into water reserves deep underground in the water table. A thick, fleshy taproot can also act as a store of energy if the plant loses its leaves.

How plants adapt to cope with drought

In areas of low rainfall, plants adapt to drought by becoming more efficient in their water use. They become more efficient at accessing, storing, and using water, as well as at preventing water loss through evaporation. Leaves can be a major source of water loss in a plant, offering a massive surface area for water to evaporate from. Some plants have evolved small leaves or needles to help prevent water loss; other plants have silver leaves to reflect heat, or hairy, woolly surfaces to provide shade. A number of eucalyptus trees have taken this evolution one step further and have developed a green bark with the ability to photosynthesize. This allows them to shed their leaves in the driest months when it is too hot for leaves to be efficient.

(top left) The hairy silver leaves of *Ballota* reflect light and heat away from the plant.

(top right) Most euphorbias have swollen, fleshy stems rather than fleshy foliage—but it does the same job.

(bottom left) The fuzzy grey-green leaves of lamb's ears help it to conserve water in extreme heat.

(bottom right) Rosemary's tiny needlelike foliage and tough skin are ways it protects itself in dry conditions. The aromatic oils also help; they increase the air density around the plant to reduce water loss by evaporation.

GREEN TIP Pale colours reflect light and heat. Use a light-coloured stone mulch 2.5 to 5 cm (1 to 2 in) deep to reduce water loss from your drought-tolerant planting scheme.

A plant's ability to adapt to local water availability is not limited to desert plants, as you might expect. All plants, from forest to grassland, show the same ability to acclimatize and make efficient use of available moisture, according to a 2004 article by Huxman et al. in *Nature*.

Many cacti have adopted a spherical shape, as this has the smallest surface area relative to volume. The succulent body of the plant has a thick, waxy skin that prevents evaporation, and the stomata open only at night to further reduce water loss through evaporation. In addition, the silver hairs and spines on the surface of the cacti reflect heat and light away from the cacti, preventing it from overheating.

Many plants have adopted fleshy leaves that actually store water, and to prevent these water reserves being lost to evaporation, these succulent leaves are often coated with a waxy or tough skin. Other plants hide their swollen water-storing bulbs or rhizomes underground, flowering in winter or spring, surviving the hottest months in a dormant state.

How to identify drought-tolerant plants

The best way to identify drought-tolerant plants is to look for the drought adaptations described in the list that follows. Some of the most drought-tolerant plants have adopted several of these tactics. Many of our favourite Mediterranean plants, for example, partner silver leaves with downy hairs and an aromatic scent.

SUCCULENT OR FLESHY FOLIAGE. The fleshy leaves and thick waxy skin of sedum and aloe vera help them conserve water even in extreme heat. Break open a piece of sedum and the thick, rubbery skin will be evident against the gooey gel of the moist inside. Most euphorbias have swollen, fleshy stems rather than fleshy foliage—but it does the same job. Other succulents to try in your drought-tolerant planting include yucca, agave, and spiderwort (*Tradescantia* species).

THICK SKIN. The thick skin of rosemary helps it conserve water even in extreme heat. Other plants with thick skin to try in your drought-tolerant planting include ceanothus, escallonia, yucca, and mahonia.

GREY, SILVER, OR GLAUCOUS LEAVES. Many drought-tolerant plants have grey, silver, or glaucous leaves to reflect light and heat. Plants with grey or silver leaves include *Eryngium giganteum* 'Silver Ghost', *Astellia chathamica* 'Silver Spear', *Lamium macculatum* 'Beacon Silver', *Thymus vulgaris* 'Silver Posie', and *Artemesia ludoviciana* 'Silver Queen'. Or try the glaucous *Festuca glauca* 'Elijah Blue', *Populus alba*, *Pyrus salicifolia* 'Pendulata', *Sorbus aria* 'Lutescens', or *Eleagnus* ×*ebbingei*.

HAIRY OR WOOLLY SURFACES. The hairy leaves of *Stachys byzantina* (lamb's ears) help them conserve water even in extreme heat by reflecting light away from the plant. Hairs on the underside of the leaf raise the humidity of the surrounding air and slow down the movement of air so that water is carried away more slowly. Other hairy plants to try in your drought-tolerant planting include *Ballota*, *Salvia officinalis* 'Berrgarten', and *Cynara cardunculus*.

AROMATIC SCENT. Have you noticed how many of the plants that are adapted to drought have aromatic leaves? Apparently, the scent of lavender is not purely for our enjoyment—it seems that the volatile oils that are produced by these aromatic plants actually increase the air density around them and reduce evaporation. Other aromatic plants to try in your drought-tolerant planting include rosemary, germander (*Teucrium*), catmint, yarrow, anise hyssop (*Agastache*), Russian sage, and *Calamintha* and *Artemesia* species.

SMALL LEAVES. The tiny leaves of hebe help make efficient use of available water by reducing evaporation. Hebe can also have fleshy, waxy leaves that store water for times of extreme drought. Other small-leaved plants to consider for your drought-tolerant planting scheme include ceanothus, thyme, rockrose (*Cistus*), and dianthus.

LEAF NEEDLES. Some plants have adopted thin, tough, waxy leaf needles in an attempt to prevent water loss by evaporation. Many of these, such as conifers, also contain volatile oils. Try *Pinus nigra*, rosemary, and lavender.

STRAPPY LEAVES. The strappy leaves of most ornamental grasses help them cope with drought by reducing water lost through evaporation. Try giant feather grass (*Stipa gigantea*), switchgrass (*Panicum*), fountain grass (*Pennisetum*), the glaucous, strappy leaves of fescue (*Festuca*), or the waxy, strappy leaves of phormium.

DEEP TAPROOTS OR SWOLLEN WATER-STORING DEVICES. Most bulbs flower in spring when water is plentiful and then become dormant during the hottest months. Try foxtail lily (*Eremurus*), tulips, and *Scilla* species.

Plants That Survive High Winds

Wind is a thief that steals the water plants need to make energy. Wind speeds up evaporation and can strip a plant of moisture in minutes. Interestingly, many of the tactics plants adopt to cope with cold winds are very similar to the modifications they make to cope with drought.

Wind poses a number of threats to the gardener. All wind strips moisture from plants, sudden gales can snap branches and stems, cold winds can "scorch" tender new growth (turning it brown and crispy),

GREEN TIP **Allow newly planted trees to move in the wind, as they will grow stronger root systems and limbs this way. Plant small for the best chance of establishment on a windy site. (Taller trees will need staking, which means they will lose the benefit of flexing as they grow.)**

and consistent windy conditions can deform plants and trees. The best way gardeners can help plants adapt to the damaging effects of wind is to slow it down by creating a windbreak, but the right plant choices will also help. Some plants do have a few tricks to cope with this fierce nemesis.

How plants adapt to cope with windy conditions

As with drought-tolerant plants, one of the best adaptations a plant can make to protect itself is to slow down the air movement that strips moisture from it. One of the best trees for windy conditions is the poplar. This sturdy tree has a regular distribution of side branches all the way up the trunk to filter and slow the wind. Unlike many standard (lollypop-shaped) trees, which shed their lower branches as they get taller, the poplar has an even spacing of branches right down to ground level. Weeping trees are also very effective at filtering wind. You can improve the ability of a tree or plant to cope with wind by planting a multi-stemmed or feathered specimen with plenty of branches.

On a smaller scale, downy or hairy leaves can help slow the air speed close to the plant while thick, waxy leaves or needles can help control moisture. The shape of smaller plants is equally important in their adaptation to windy conditions. As with drought-tolerant plants, a low, rounded shape (with reduced surface area) helps plants retain moisture even on windy sites.

One of the problems with windy conditions is that they can be very unpredictable. A strong wind can arise without warning, so plants need to be ready for a surprise attack. A strong, deep root system provides an essential anchor, while above the ground, flexibility is important. Flexible stems and wide-spreading branches are key to avoiding damage from a fast, whipping wind. Trees need to have strong, flexible branches that do not snap easily, while grasses and perennials need to be able to bend almost flat to the ground in windy conditions before springing upright, undamaged, when the wind calms. *Calamagrostis* is particularly good at coping with sudden windstorms and can handle winds of up to 80 mph.

How to identify wind-tolerant plants

The best way to identify wind-tolerant plants is to look for the adaptations described in the list that follows. Plants adapted for wind toler-

The direction from which the wind most often blows will influence your garden's character and what you can grow. As a general rule, northerlies and easterlies are cold, while westerlies are warmer but stronger.

ance can be harder to spot than their drought-tolerant counterparts, although many characteristics are shared. The overall plant shape is important, so try to see a mature specimen when choosing trees and shrubs.

FLEXIBLE STEMS AND BRANCHES. Flexible stems and branches help plants move with the wind and reduce the damage a sudden gust might cause. Try *Pinus flexilis*, which has branches so supple they can be bent double without breaking. Other limber choices include hazel and willow (after all, we know they are flexible enough for weaving). Ornamental grasses are almost universally flexible. If you are spoilt for choice, start with *Calamagrostis* or *Stipa*.

THICK, WAXY LEAVES, OR NEEDLES. Conifers are a great choice for a windy site as their tough, waxy needles help prevent water loss by evaporation. The best choice of conifer will depend on your location. Good bets to try include fir, larch, or spruce. Alternatively, plants with thick, waxy, evergreen leaves such as Holm oak and holly cope well with a windy site. The same principles work just as well when choosing smaller wind-tolerant plants for your garden. The needlelike foliage of heathers, such as *Calluna* and *Erica*, makes them a good bet—as do the thick, waxy leaves of *Eleagnus* ×*ebbingei* or *Bergenia*.

GOOD DISTRIBUTION OF BRANCHES TO FILTER THE WIND. Weeping trees such as willow, weeping birch, and weeping hornbeam (*Carpinus betulus* 'Pendula') help filter the wind with their drooping branches. Try also *Cornus alba* 'Elegantissima' (or any of the dogwoods), poplar, and alder.

LOW, ROUNDED SHAPE OR LOW CENTRE OF GRAVITY. A low, rounded shape or low centre of gravity helps plants avoid wind damage. Juniper, with its low spreading branches and thin needles, is a good example. Try also the low-growing Mugo pine or the ubiquitous heather.

Shelterbelts and windbreaks

The idea with a shelterbelt is not to stop the wind completely but to slow it down. Putting up a solid barrier, such as a wall or close-boarded fence, can actually make the problem worse. The wind is forced up and over the barrier; then it dips down and eddies at the base of the wall. A

GREEN TIP **Poplars are excellent at slowing the wind on exposed sites as they have branches that start at the very base of the trunk and are evenly distributed along its length, effectively helping to slow the wind.**

Mugo pine avoids wind damage because of its low centre of gravity.

far better choice is a semi-permeable structure, such as a double-sided fence, shrubs, trees, or hedges. Depending on the space you have available, there will be a solution to suit you.

A simple rule to remember is to site your shelterbelt as far away from the area you are protecting as the mature height of the plants. A 2-m (6-ft) hedge need only be planted 3 m (9 ft) from the area you are protecting (this allows 1 m or 3 ft either side of the hedge centre to allow for the width of the mature hedge), whereas poplars should be planted at least 28 m (90 ft) away. A successful windbreak should extend beyond the width of the area you are intending to shelter so that you are protected from a change in wind direction.

When designing a windbreak, avoid plantings that use only one type of plant, as disease affecting a single species can quickly wipe out all your hard work. It is better to plant an odd number of trees in staggered rows. Site the tallest trees facing immediately into the prevailing winds, followed by progressively smaller trees. Poplar and hazel are good choices as they have evenly spread branches that do not die lower down as the tree matures.

Fast-growing plants can be important in very windy sites. At East Ruston Old Vicarage in north Norfolk, a shelterbelt of fast-growing *Pinus radiata*, *Alnus cordata*, and *Eucalyptus coccifera* has created a microclimate just 3 km (roughly 2 miles) from the North Sea in which tropical plants thrive and self-seed.

GARDEN ON A WINDY SITE IN NOTTINGHAMSHIRE

I was commissioned to design a new garden in Nottinghamshire on a very windy site—so windy that the bricks on the northwest corner of the house have been worn to a smooth curve by the prevailing wind. I knew the key to the design was to slow the wind down and create sheltered pockets of open space without making the garden feel too enclosed.

The first job was to include hedges along the boundary. These served the dual purpose of screening out the neighbours' shed and slowing the wind. A row of pleached hornbeam was planted in combination with a low hornbeam hedge to further filter the wind and frame the view out into the landscape.

The planting in this area was a matrix of sturdy ornamental grasses and later-flowering perennials. Forty percent of the grasses were *Calamagrostis* ×*acutiflora* 'Karl Foerster', an ornamental grass well known for its tolerance of strong winds. *Panicum virgatum* 'Heavy Metal', another wind-tolerant grass with clouds of russet seedheads, was also included in the matrix.

One of the cheapest and best windbreaks available to the gardener is a hedge. Hedges create a dense tangle of branches, which slow down the wind and trap air to insulate a garden. Hornbeam is a good choice for shelterbelt hedging because it grows quickly, and although it is deciduous it holds its leaves over the winter. Another excellent choice is a mixed native hedge. Try 25 percent hawthorn and 25 percent blackthorn mixed with dogwood, hazel, euonymus, crab apple, viburnum, and species roses. In coastal gardens, plants will have to deal with salt as well as wind, so you would be better off installing a hedge of escallonia or *Rosa rugosa* 'Roseraie de L'Hay'.

Foundation planting

Traditionally a border of shrubs was planted all around the house to disguise the concrete footings or foundations. Construction techniques have changed and foundation planting has been out of fashion for some years now, but it might be worth reconsidering for the insulating benefits it can offer us. We have already seen how windbreaks can slow and trap air, and foundation planting follows the same principles. Plant evergreens around the house, leaving a 1.5-m (5-ft) gap between the planting and the property (to trap air), and you will insulate your home in the winter and help keep it cool in the summer.

GREEN TIP Site your shelterbelt as far away from the area you are protecting as the mature height of the plants. Plant an odd number of trees in staggered rows and avoid using just one type of tree.

Plant evergreens around the foundation of your home to insulate it in the winter and keep it cool in the summer. Leave a gap of 1.5 m (5 ft) between the plants and the house to trap air.

Calamagrostis ×*acutiflora* can withstand winds of up to 80 miles per hour. This versatile ornamental grass will revert to healthy upright growth even after being bent horizontal by strong winds.

Plants with a degree of flood tolerance

GRASSES
- *Arundo donax*
- *Deschampsia cespitosa*

TREES
- *Alnus rubra* and *A. glutinosa*
- *Betula nigra* and *B. pendula*
- *Carpinus betulus*
- *Fraxinus excelsior*
- *Liquidambar styraciflua*
- *Taxodium distichum*

SHRUBS
- *Cornus sanguinea*
- *Ilex verticillata*
- *Ribes nigrum*
- *Salix caprea* and other *Salix* species
- *Sambucus nigra*
- *Viburnum opulus*

PERENNIALS
- *Aster novae-angliae*
- *Filipendula purpurea*
- *Hemerocallis* species
- *Hosta* species
- *Iris pseudacorus* and *I. sibirica*
- *Lythrum salicaria*
- *Viola pedata*

Plants to Withstand High Rainfall and Flooding

When soil becomes waterlogged, plants cannot extract from it the oxygen they need; this is called anoxia. As a general rule, plants will not survive without oxygen for more than three days, but flood-tolerant plants have developed mechanisms to cope.

How plants adapt to cope with wet conditions

Plants lack a circulatory system, so they cannot move oxygen from the air to their roots. Instead, the roots get their oxygen from root spaces in the soil around them. The rate of diffusion of oxygen is much faster in air (as a gas) than in water. When the soil becomes waterlogged, the roots struggle to get the oxygen they need. Marsh plants have aerenchyma tissue; these are air spaces in the stems that transport oxygen from the leaves to the roots. This can be by simple diffusion or by active pressure, depending on the plant.

The process that all organisms, including plants, use to gain energy is known as respiration. When there is enough oxygen available, this is called aerobic respiration. When oxygen is limited, plants must turn to anaerobic respiration. The main drawbacks of anaerobic respiration are that it is less energy efficient and that toxic by-products build up and the plant must expend even more energy in getting rid of them. In humans this is lactic acid, but in plants this tends to be alcohols, including ethanol.

Research has shown that flood-tolerant plants can respond to these toxic metabolites by increasing breakdown enzymes such as alcohol dehydrogenase or ADH.

How to identify flood-tolerant plants

Unfortunately, there are no hard-and-fast rules for identifying flood-tolerant plants. One way to choose flood-tolerant plants is to look for them in their natural habitats, such as marsh or the margins of watercourses—but a lot of it is trial and error. Research is ongoing and there is no one source of information on this topic.

9

Substituting New Alternatives for Classic Favourites

The changeable weather we have been enduring has highlighted the need for a new approach to our planting choices. In previous years we would label gardens as "reliably moist" or "subject to drought" with some ease and then plant them accordingly, but things are becoming less and less predictable. Weather extremes of flood and drought now occur without warning, often within a period of days. If we can no longer rely on the accepted weather cycles of the past, we will need to adapt our planting schemes to cope with unpredictable and volatile weather.

Gardening in a changing climate requires us to look for storm-tolerant alternatives to our favourite plants so that we can continue to design with trees and blossoms and fragrance. For the unpredictable weather challenges ahead, we will need to develop a sophisticated arsenal of bimodal plants—that is, plants that can cope with more than one type of weather extreme. Luckily, there are a number of multi-tolerant plants that offer similar characteristics to our garden design favourites.

Bimodal Plants by Category

First we will look at trees, woody shrubs, ornamental grasses, and shrubs that can tolerate weather extremes. Curiously, plants that typically grow in moist habitats often survive rather well in drier soils (as long as the soil is reasonably fertile), but the opposite is rarely true. Plants that are adapted to dry conditions often struggle to cope with flooding and waterlogged soils.

Trees

We have already examined the essential role trees play in the health of the planet, but trees are equally important from a design point of view. They introduce height and a sense of permanence into a garden, offering shelter as well as screening or framing the landscape beyond. Many trees are unable to cope with the oscillating weather conditions we are beginning to experience, and beech and cherry are known to be particularly vulnerable to flooding. A sensible landscaping choice would be to substitute storm-tolerant alternatives that offer similar visual characteristics.

Rather than struggling to keep beech healthy in times of stress, why not try using hornbeam as an alternative for trees and hedges? Horn-

GREEN TIP **Avoid alpines, beech, *Prunus* species (including plums, cherries, peaches, apricots), and other fruit trees in the storm-tolerant garden.**

Recommended bimodal trees

- *Acer saccharinum*
- *Alnus glutinosa*
- *Amelanchier* species
- *Betula nigra*
- *Carpinus* species
- *Crataegus* species
- *Eucalyptus robusta*
- *Fraxinus* species
- *Liquidambar styraciflua*
- *Salix* species

(top) Eastern redbud (*Cercis canadensis*) can be grown as a tree or a pollarded shrub for its wonderful heart-shaped purple foliage.

(center) Try a bimodal woodland shrub such as *Hydrangea quercifolia* in place of the fussy camellia.

(bottom) Black currant (*Ribes nigrum*) is a shrub that offers spring blossoms, fall berries, and tolerance of both flooding and drought.

GREEN TIP **Avoid hellebores, *Primula vialii*, tiarella, camellia, and forsythia, which do not cope well with waterlogged soil.**

Recommended bimodal woodland plants

- *Acuba japonica*
- *Aquilegia* species
- *Asplenium* species
- *Baptisia* species
- *Berberis thunbergii*
- *Brunnera* species
- *Convallaria majalis*
- *Cornus mas*
- *Dryopteris filix-mas*
- *Fatsia japonica*
- *Hydrangea quercifolia*
- *Liriope* species
- *Primula veris*
- *Primula vulgaris*
- *Viburnum tinus*
- *Viola pedata*

OTHER RECOMMENDED
BIMODAL SHRUBS
- *Cercis canadensis*
- *Hebe* species
- *Hibiscus moscheutos*
- *Physocarpus opulifolius*
- *Ribes nigrum*
- *Rosa canina*
- *Rosa rugosa*
- *Viburnum dentate*

beam can tolerate wind, drought, and flooding but is visually very similar to beech. As an alternative to the cherry tree, plant serviceberry (*Amelanchier*), which offers clouds of spring blossoms that are always a joy. Serviceberry also provides exquisite autumn colour—and if planted as a multi-stem specimen can act as a miniwindbreak. An alternative source of storm-tolerant autumn colour can be found in the form of the vibrantly coloured *Liquidambar styraciflua* or *Acer saccharinum*—both of which tolerate extremes of flood and drought with some ease.

Few trees, except the large swamp cypress (*Taxodium distichum*), can tolerate more than one month of submersion during the growing season. But as a general rule, broad-leaved trees tolerate flooding better than conifers. Try alder, river birch (*Betula nigra*), hornbeam, willow, and ash for your best chance of success.

Woodland plants

Few woody shrubs are any better adapted to flooded conditions than trees. Common casualties of extreme weather conditions include forsythia, daphne, camellias, and yew, which simply panic in waterlogged soil. These can be grown in a pot or replaced by plants that can more effectively tolerate volatile weather conditions. We can probably all think of a few "hard as nails" shrubs, such as *Fatsia japonica* and *Viburnum tinus*, that can tolerate almost anything you throw at them, but wouldn't it be boring if these were our only options for storm-tolerant shrubs? Eastern redbud (*Cercis canadensis*), one of my all-time favourite planting choices, is surprisingly storm tolerant—and can cope with long-term drought as well as a good few days of standing water. Rose mallow (*Hibiscus moscheutos*) is another fantastically elegant shrub that is suspiciously hard to kill.

Cornelian cherry dogwood (*Cornus mas*) and Japanese barberry (*Berberis thunbergii*) are two other shrubs commonly reported to be tolerant of flooding, even during the growing season. An ideal storm- and flood-tolerant plant partner for your dogwood would be *Asplenium* species, liriope, columbine (*Aquilegia*), or male fern (*Dryopteris filix-mas*). Lily of the valley (*Convallaria majalis*) is another woodland perennial that survives both drought and flooding, but it is remarkably invasive and can be hard to control in a planting scheme so is a less ideal choice on a domestic garden scale. Avoid hellebores and tiarella entirely as they do not cope well with waterlogged soil.

(top left) Columbine (*Aquilegia*) partners well with dogwood in the storm-tolerant garden.

(top right) Lily of the valley is multi-tolerant and provides great scent—but it can be rather invasive if left unchecked.

(bottom left) The storm-tolerant glossy evergreen fronds of *Asplenium* species are particularly useful as a foil.

(bottom right) Avoid *Primula vialli*. *P. veris* and *P. vulgaris* are much more tolerant of unpredictable weather conditions.

Many of the plants we have traditionally used to fulfill these requirements thrive only in certain conditions; astrantias require reliably moist soil, while yews hate to have wet feet and sulk in standing water. The storm-tolerant garden will rely on the same pieces of the jigsaw puzzle as traditional plantings; we will still focus on plants that will do a job for us in the planting scheme, but we may have to think harder to find plants that will cope with the stresses of both drought and flooding. Here are some multi-tolerant alternatives for common purposes or situations.

Spring blossoms

Nothing quite stirs the heart like a cloud of spring blossoms. In Japan, the annual cherry blossom viewings, hanami, have been taking place since the seventh century and I have to admit I'm just as susceptible to the delicate froth of blossom that arrives each spring. *Prunus* species are among the most popular choices for spring blossoms, but they really hate flooding, so they will be of little use in the storm-tolerant garden. For a dazzling show of blossoms, try *Amelanchier* species instead. These have spectacular white clouds of blossoms in spring and can withstand several weeks of drought and a good few days of standing water.

Evergreen foliage

When designing a planting scheme, I usually start by thinking about the winter framework. I use evergreen plants and structural trees and shrubs to form a skeleton for the garden. This winter structure has to hold its own before I begin to flesh it out with other plantings. Repeating blocks of evergreen planting is a classic device used to bring structure and cohesion to planting schemes. They play a particularly important role in providing bulk to schemes that are dominated by perennials. Many of the toughest plants are evergreens, and you will be spoilt for choice finding evergreen plants that will tolerate a degree of wind, flood, and drought.

For evergreen structure and bulk, try *Aucuba japonica* or *Fatsia japonica*. Camellias require a steady supply of moisture throughout the summer months when their buds are developing if they are to put on a good show of flowers in the spring. A better choice for the storm-tolerant garden might be *Viburnum tinus*, whose shiny green leaves are complemented by a winter showing of tiny scented flowers.

(top left) Despite its silvery leaves, this *Eleagnus ×ebbingei* is surprisingly tolerant of wet conditions.

(top right) Hebe is a really useful evergreen that is available in every scale from mini to mighty.

(bottom left) Try Japanese barberry for clipped hedges and topiary.

(bottom right) Photinia is a tough storm-tolerant shrub that can be usefully trained as a half standard or pleached hedge.

GREEN TIP **Avoid boxwood (*Buxus*) wherever possible, as it is increasingly under attack from the fungal infection box blight. Instead try the storm-tolerant *Teucrium ×lucidrys* for low hedges and small topiary shapes.**

Clipping and topiary

Evergreens give winter structure to the garden, but few things offset the loose riot of perennial planting better than some neatly clipped topiary. Traditional topiary plants include boxwood (*Buxus*) and yew (*Taxus*). For knot gardens, santolina, rosemary, and hebe also make an appearance. As we have already discovered, most grey- and silver-leaved plants hate flooding, so santolina and rosemary will be no good in the storm-tolerant garden. A better choice for a low clipped hedge would be barberry or *Teucrium ×lucidrys*.

Yew will also suffer in the storm-tolerant garden. Notorious for hating wet feet, yew will be killed off by even a short time in standing water. There are plenty of other dense, slow-growing evergreens that can be used as a substitute for yew topiary. Try clipping holly or myrtle into bold topiary shapes. Try using hornbeam or photinia to create pleached hedges, or try growing an evergreen climber over a wire frame to similar effect.

Architectural foliage

Architectural foliage is also useful to give structure to a planting. The swordlike foliage of iris and phormium can provide an invaluable bold accent in contrast to the more rounded shapes of shrubs and hedges. Iris are some of my favourite plants because they work so hard in a planting scheme. The crisp blades of foliage work like spires, leading the eye skyward and providing an important contrast to the billowing spring foliage around them. The tightly wrapped buds remind me of the flint arrowheads on a spear, and the irises are an equally commanding presence. When the velvety flowers finally open, the dynamic shifts from the architectural foliage to the opulent flowers. Sadly, wet soils can cause the more showy *Iris germanica* corms to rot in the planting bed, so a better choice would be *Iris sibirica*, whose more refined foliage is more akin to that of ornamental grasses. *Iris sibirica* can be used as a marginal plant and copes well with flooding and some shade. It also copes very well in dry soil in full sun, so put it on the list for your storm-tolerant garden.

The low, crinkled foliage of heuchera is a favourite with garden designers because of its clean architectural shape, reliable foliage, and ability to cope with all levels of moisture. On a larger scale, the giant textured leaves of rodgersia offer a distinctive outline but are only reliable in moist soil.

Winter fragrance

The alluring scent of a winter-flowering shrub is one of the things I look forward to most on a crisp, cold day. It can be tempting to abandon a garden over the winter months, to stay inside, light a fire, and wait until spring—so it's especially important to include plants that will tempt you out into the winter garden. Winter-flowering plants often have small delicate flowers, flowers you could almost miss if it were not for their beguiling scent. It's a clever trick—after all, you wouldn't be so persuaded to go out and enjoy the crisp winter's day if you could appreciate the plants from the window, now would you?

Daphnes are a classic winter-flowering choice, but they are a bit too fussy for the storm-tolerant garden. Their heady fragrance comes at a price, for they hate being too wet (especially over the summer months), they don't cope well in dry conditions, and they hate being exposed to the hot sun, plus they are prone to dieback even in the most ideal conditions. A better choice for winter fragrance in the storm-tolerant garden would be *Sarcococca*. From the large glossy leaves of *S. confusa* to the compact *S. hookeriana* var. *digyna*, you will be spoilt for choice.

Oregon grape (*Mahonia aquifolium*) is another hardworking winter-scented shrub to consider in the storm-tolerant garden. With large evergreen hollylike leaves that take on a red-purple tint in cold weather, bright yellow winter flowers, sweet fragrance, and spring berries, mahonia would seem to tick all the boxes, but you might want to save this plant for use as an evergreen ground cover as it does have a tendency to sucker. I am not a fan of bright yellow flowers, though, so the choice I return to time and time again is *Viburnum ×bodnatense* 'Dawn', which has blush-pink flowers on bare stems. Although deciduous, this viburnum offers gorgeous autumn colour and makes an excellent cut stem to bring indoors.

Winter colour

Winter colour is also important in the garden, although our choices are limited at the best of times. Luckily, many of the classics are very tolerant of unpredictable weather conditions and are well adapted to cope with both wet and dry conditions.

Willow is always a good choice for winter colour. Try golden willow (*Salix alba* var. *vitellina*). Alternatively, you will find it hard to go far wrong with the dogwoods *Cornus sanguinea* or *Cornus sericea*. Plants to avoid include *Hamamellis* (witch hazel) and *Skimmia japonica*.

GREEN TIP **Consider choosing the improved *Mahonia aquifolium* 'Apollo', which has been awarded the prestigious Award of Garden Merit (AGM) by the Royal Horticultural Society, over the straight variety.**

Spires

Spires are among the most dominant shapes in a mixed planting. There is something almost reverential in the way they lead the eye up out of the border and into the heavens. Spires rebel against the round shapes of most other plants and add sharp definition and contrast to a planting.

Spires can take many forms: sometimes a cluster of tightly packed flowers up a slender, linear stem, like *Salvia* 'May Night', other times a series of whorls like phlomis. One of the most reliable spires for the storm-tolerant garden is red bistort (*Persicaria amplexicaulis*). Admittedly, its foliage is a bit butch and uninspiring (some say it looks a bit like a dock leaf), but it flowers on and on and on in all conditions.

Some spires, such as foxglove, have one single, statuesque thrust of blooms reaching skyward. The individual flowers may be large and the effect bold and towering, but they can often be top-heavy and require staking. Avoid the overbearing demands of traditional herbaceous spires that require watering, staking, and protection from slugs by replacing top-heavy lupines and delphiniums with spires that have more natural proportions (so are more able to fend for themselves) such as the hooded flowers of wild indigo (*Baptisia*) or monkshood (*Aconitum*).

Some spires are made up of a series of smaller spires. I love these complex spires above all others but my absolute favourite, *Veronicastrum*, is so prone to midday wilting that blue vervain (*Verbena hastata*) or the simple spires of gayfeather (*Liatris spicata*) would be a more reliable choice.

Buttons and globes

Buttons and globes represent the biggest group of plants. They can be large perfect globes of spiky flowers, such as echinops, or a peppering of tiny buttons, such as burnet (*Sanguisorba*). Confusingly, many buttons are also a veil, such as the haze of wiry stems of knautia topped with pincushion flowers. Whatever the size, these daubs of colour sing out from a planting scheme. Buttons punctuate plantings in a vast array of colours, from the soft yellow of sulphur clover (*Trifolium ochroleucon*) to the intense shots of bee balm (*Monarda*). In the winter the number of buttons increases as daisies such as echinacea lose their petals and join the other buttons.

(above) The grand spires of phlomis, here with seedheads, are made up of a series of whorls.

(top left) The natural proportions of monkshood (*Aconitum*) means you don't have to stake these plants.

(center left) *Salvia nemorosa* 'Wesuwe' is great for the front of the border.

(bottom left) Persicaria has long flowering spires in white, pink, or red. Just be sure to hide the boring foliage with other planting.

You don't have to sacrifice buttons and globes when planning your storm-tolerant planting scheme. In place of the capricious bee balm (which is unhappy in soil that is either too wet or too dry), try the reliable petalfree globes of western coneflower (*Rudbeckia occidentalis*) or the blue globes of echinops—which are tolerant to a fault. Burnet, first choice for a daubing of button-shaped flowers, is another case in point. Since this prefers a reliably moist soil, common bistort (*Persicaria bistorta*) or knautia might be a better choice.

Daisies

A billowing mass of dainty daisies can add bulk to a planting, while larger daisies (perhaps echinaceas) act more like buttons and make a more defined exclamation. Daisies are striking plants that always seem to cheer up a garden. They are usually found in a sunny spot and infuse a planting with vitality from early summer right through until late autumn. As the winter draws in, many daisies lose their petals, punching through the bleached-out border with buttons of dark coffee.

Ox-eye and Shasta daisies (*Leucanthemum* species) are probably the most classic daisy flower for the herbaceous border. Pure white petals surround a bright yellow centre for consistent flowers in all weather conditions. *Leucanthemum ×superbum* 'T. E. Killin' is perhaps the best known, flowering at 70 cm (28 in) high, but the shorter *Leucanthemum ×superbum* 'Snowcap' should also be on the storm-tolerant planting list. The gardener is spoilt for storm-tolerant choice with daisy-shaped flowers: rudbeckia, echinacea, and anthemis are all reliably profuse. Asters are another good choice, although I give *Aster frikartii* 'Monch' the highest rating.

Veils

Whether it's a mass of branching stems or dense, fluffy clouds, veils always bring a romantic and ephemeral mood to a planting. The open, transparent habit of veils allows you to break a few rules. Rather than keeping the taller plants at the back of the border, veils allow you to place taller specimens at the front or middle of a bed, teasing you to look beyond while allowing the sunlight to stream through. A vapour of *Crambe cordifolia* is a dynamic foil for the more precise, elegant outline of a bold spire or daisy, and its smaller cousin, sea kale (*Crambe maritima*) makes a useful transparent screen at the front of the border.

Spring flower spikes of heuchera and fringe cups create the same type of effect at the front of the border.

Ornamental grasses make some of the most useful veils in the storm-tolerant garden. Perhaps the most popular of these veiling grasses is *Molinia* 'Transparent', a hot favourite among garden designers. The airy, almost transparent flowers stand upright and create an almost transparent screen, an effect that is only enhanced by morning dew or a quick shower of rain.

Edging plants

The best edging plants are compact and neat, so there is often an emphasis on reliable foliage. They need to be delicate enough to balance the showier plants in the border, yet tough enough to look good whatever the weather throws at them. Some gardeners choose to install a uniform edging plant along the whole border, but I worry this can look rather forced. I prefer to use a combination of two or three edging plants repeated in a random pattern so that the edging looks neat but as if it could have spontaneously seeded.

Catmint (*Nepeta*) is a popular edging plant, but it doesn't cope well with flooding and dies back in the winter months. A better choice might be *Ajuga reptans*, since its evergreen purple-bronze foliage seems happy in drought and flood. Ajuga has lovely short spires of purple flowers in the spring that are very popular with beneficial insects. Epimedium is another multi-tolerant contender that will add colour to even the shadiest spot.

Climbing plants

When planning your planting, don't forget to consider the vertical plants. Climbers are a great way to add height to your garden. Climbers offer lush foliage and real height in only a couple of seasons and can be a useful way to make a garden feel mature even while more slowly growing trees and shrubs are growing to their full height.

Wisteria is one of the most popular choices to climb a garden wall or the side of a house—but it is also one of the fussiest. An alternative summer-flowering climber such as *Hydrangea petiolaris* would be a better choice for the storm-tolerant garden. Roses are also popular, and although all species shrub roses like *Rosa rugosa* and *Rosa nutkana* 'Plena' are pretty storm-tolerant choices, I have yet to find a climbing

(top left) Ajuga is a robust edging plant that will tolerate almost any conditions. The glossy purple leaves are an asset to any planting scheme.

(top right) Calamint makes a lovely frothy edging to a border.

(bottom left) Epimedium is useful in sun or shade and the leaves stay on right through the winter months. Cut them back in spring if you want to reveal the dainty flowers.

(bottom right) The evergreen strappy leaves of liriope make a shade-tolerant ground cover or border edging.

rose that copes well with flood and drought. When it comes to vines, Virginia creeper (*Parthenocissus quinquefolia*) is a more tolerant choice than a grapevine such as *Vitis vinifera* 'Purpurea'.

Autumn colour

As the splendour of summer draws to a close and the days get shorter, the colours of the garden begin to bleach out to ashen, ochre, and browns. Then all of a sudden, the leaves begin to turn and we are rewarded with a fiery display of autumn colour. Despite the inevitable disappointment that the end of summer brings, I am always excited when autumn begins to kick in. Perhaps it is because the change in leaf colour coincides with my birthday, or perhaps it's just the joy of all this colour.

As with blossom, *Prunus* species are a popular choice for reliable autumn colour, but *Prunus* really doesn't cope well with flooding. *Liquidambar styraciflua* (American sweetgum) is a better choice for the storm-tolerant garden.

Staghorn sumac (*Rhus typhina*) is another excellent choice for storm-tolerant autumn colour. It copes well with drought, high winds, and a certain amount of flooding, and the autumn leaf colour is simply breathtaking. Sumac spreads by suckering, so it is usually worth containing the roots with a barrier, just like you would do with bamboo.

Hedges

Unless you skipped over chapter 5, you will already know how much I love hedges. They are inexpensive to install, they slow the wind, they benefit wildlife, and they need very little love and attention throughout the year in terms of pruning. Hedges are an important part of any garden scheme. They provide structure to the garden, creating garden rooms, enclosing spaces, and framing views. Hedges provide an essential foil for planting, whether you are planning a simple scheme dominated by trees and shrubs or a more blowsy perennial planting.

Because beech hates flooding, grow your hedges out of hornbeam instead. Hornbeam is an excellent choice for a hedge as it can cope with drought, wind, and flood. Beech and hornbeam look very similar to the naked eye; the main difference is that hornbeam leaves have a serrated edge, whereas beech leaves have a softer wave to them.

You don't have to stick to the classics when planning your hedge. Many flowering shrubs can be grown as a hedge. In France, lilac is a

(above) The transluscent red berries of *Viburnum opulus* are popular with gardeners and birds—and the autumn colour is also attractive.

(right) The spectacular colours of liquidambar (sweetgum) will draw you in from a distance.

(next page top) Try *Hydrangea quercifolia* for giant spires of summer flowers and vibrant autumn colour.

(next page bottom) If space is limited, add autumn colour with a climber, such as this lovely Virginia creeper (*Parthenocissus quinquefolia*).

popular choice for an informal hedge, but since it doesn't like getting its feet wet, *Viburnum tinus* or *Rosa rugosa* is a better choice. I was excited to come across hibiscus hedges in the gardens at Filoli near San Francisco, and I was cross that I hadn't thought of using this storm-tolerant shrub as a hedge myself.

Lawn

Any gardener knows how easy it is to damage a traditional lawn. If the weather is wet, you can wear lawn into a muddy track. Walking on a snow-covered lawn can be equally damaging, and lack of water will turn it brown and crispy. We also know how brilliant lawns are at recovering; they quickly green up after a bit of rain, and if allowed to seed, they will patch themselves. A better choice for the storm-tolerant garden might be a lawn of Dutch white clover (*Trifolium repens*), which stays green even at the height of summer drought and can also tolerate plenty of water. A bonus is that it fixes nitrogen in your soil and feeds the bees.

10

Gardening with Wildlife in Mind

From backyards to balconies, from courtyards to country acres, gardens form a huge network of green space that is invaluable to wildlife. Whether we are talking about pollinating insects, earthworms, or a balance between predators and prey, wildlife is essential for a healthy garden, and no garden is too small to contribute. It used to be thought that the only way to garden successfully was to dominate nature: to kill pests, to deadhead plants, and to stick to a rigid timetable of tasks. I'm not saying all gardeners have now become soft (I can think of plenty of gardeners who relish squashing the odd greedy snail underfoot), but slowly we have come to realize that gardening doesn't have to be a constant battle with nature.

Gardeners invariably have a far easier time of it if they work with nature, not against it. Aphids can be kept in check by lacewings and ladybirds (ladybugs to those in North America), and slugs can be controlled by nematodes and hungry birds. Gardeners are beginning to learn the tricks they need to tempt natural predators to make a home in their garden year-round—for example, by providing plants with winter berries so that birds have plenty to eat over the winter months when tasty slugs are less available. This chapter will teach you more ways to make your garden friendly to birds, bees, butterflies, and other beneficial insects.

Biodiversity in Urban Gardens

Even if you have only a small urban garden or a window ledge, you can make a valuable contribution to the biodiversity of your area. Remember, your garden does not exist in isolation; it's part of a wider jigsaw puzzle. In the same way that an apple tree in a neighbouring garden might pollinate the fruit in your yard, many animals will come to regard your garden as part of a wider habitat.

The garden is not just a room outside. It has a far more complex set of requirements than the style of furniture. When planning a garden, remember to provide for the insect and microbial activity that will keep your garden healthy. Even the most formal gardens have room to include an area where plants are left standing in the winter, where dead wood is stacked to provide a habitat for insects and other animals. Leaving grasses and perennials to stand over the winter will also provide a food source in the form of seed heads.

GREEN TIP **Avoid monocultural plantings that encourage pests and diseases. Instead, aim for as much diversity in your planting as possible.**

(top left) Ornamental seed heads display the fading beauty of flowering plants right into the winter. Umbels such as this *Angelica gigas* have a particularly spectactular winter skeleton.

(top right) The dried seed heads of poppies are almost as beautiful as the flowers themselves.

(middle left) It's not just sunflower seeds that will attract birds to your garden; the seed heads of flowering perennials such as echinops are also an important winter food source for birds.

(bottom left) Leaving the seed heads of asters over the winter will provide a food source for birds.

Plants with berries

SPRING
- *Mahonia* species
- *Sarcococca* species

SUMMER
- *Amelanchier* species
- *Cornus alba* and *C. florida*
- *Crataegus* species
- *Prunus* species
- *Rhamnus californica* species
- *Sambucus* species
- *Vaccinium* species
- *Viburnum* species, especially *V. opulus*

AUTUMN
- *Aronia* species
- *Berberis* species
- *Callicarpa bodinieri* (plant at least three for reliable fruiting)
- *Cotoneaster* species
- *Euonymus* species
- *Ligustrum* species
- *Lonicera* species
- *Malus* species (including crab apples)
- *Pyracantha* species
- *Rosa* species (if grown for hips— for example, *Rosa rugosa*, *R. moyesii*, *R. canina*, *R. rubiginosa*, *R. glauca*)
- *Sorbus aria*
- *Sorbus aucuparia*

WINTER
- *Ilex* species
- *Taxus baccata*
- *Viburnum tinus*, *V. davidii*

Birds

Birds help the gardener in many ways. Small birds such as the robin, wren, and tits help to control insect pests; song thrushes feed on snails; while starlings, blackbirds, robins, ducks, and even owls will enjoy your garden slugs. Finches and sparrows love seeds and will reduce weed seeds by eating them up. To encourage these helpful predators to visit your garden, you need to create a safe habitat and provide plenty of food, especially in the leaner winter months. Luckily the range of planting these birds enjoys fits well with the design considerations and aesthetics of the modern garden designer.

Bird-friendly planting

To attract birds, make sure your garden offers spiky plants, hedges, plants with berries, plants with winter interest, evergreen shrubs and conifers, and climbing plants.

SPIKY PLANTS are great for burglarproofing a garden, and birds love them for their protective qualities, too. Many small birds choose to nest in dense, spiky shrubs, such as barberry and holly, where they are safe from their predators.

HEDGES, especially those with a dense branch structure, provide places for smaller birds to nest while serving as great boundaries and dividers.

PLANTS WITH BERRIES are favored by garden designers for their extended season of interest and their jewel-like colours. Berries are also an important source of food for birds, especially in the autumn and winter when food is scarce. Shrubs bearing berries should not be cut back until late winter or after the berries have been eaten.

PLANTS WITH WINTER INTEREST have an important role to play in garden design, and a number of these derive their status from colourful berries. Winter is a time when food sources for birds are limited, so berrying winter shrubs and trees such as yews and viburnums are key.

EVERGREEN SHRUBS AND CONIFERS give year-round structure to a garden. They also provide insulation and protection from cold winds, and many birds will choose them as nesting sites.

VIGOROUS CLIMBING PLANTS such as clematis and honeysuckle are a great choice for compact gardens. Green foliage softens the boundary and can make the garden look bigger, while also providing food, shelter, and nesting spots for birds.

It is important to choose plants that provide garden birds with food throughout the year. Late summer and autumn are particularly important times to provide seeds and berries for birds as they build up their fat reserves for the winter months ahead. At this time of year, the gardener is spoilt for choice with trees and shrubs laden with berries.

Typically birds eat the brightest coloured berries and hips first, so if you find that your berries are being guzzled before you get a chance to enjoy them, it is worth including a range of different coloured berries in your planting scheme. Try the translucent orange berries of *Viburnum opulus* 'Xanthocarpum', the creamy white berries of the snowberry (*Symphoricarpos*), or one of the array of rowan species with coloured berries—for example, *Sorbus* 'Joseph Rock' (yellow berries), *S. cashmeriana* (white berries), or *S.* 'Eastern Promise' (rose-coloured berries).

Mature trees and hedges provide some of the most valuable garden habitats for birds; they offer food, shelter, and nesting opportunities (including holes). As well as providing fruit and nuts, such as berries and acorns, large trees teem with insects. If your garden is not big enough for a tree, then a hedge is equally good for birds. The dense branches of hedges and shrubs can provide nesting sites and materials for small garden birds, as can some of the more vigorous climbing plants such as clematis, ivy, and honeysuckle.

Winter feeding

In winter, natural food resources are scarce, so you may choose to provide additional food in the form of fat balls or seeds. Once you start providing this additional food, don't stop. The birds quickly come to rely on the food you put out and make a special journey to your garden to eat. If feeding is sporadic, they waste their limited energy stores looking for food and this makes winter survival even harder. A variety of food, whether offered on bird tables or in seed feeders, will attract the greatest range of species. If you are using bird feeders that have been designed with flexible perches so that only the smallest of birds can

GREEN TIP Include a range of different colours of berries in your planting scheme. Birds typically eat the brightest ones first, so don't be surprised if these disappear before you have a chance to enjoy the colour.

Plants that produce seeds

- *Aster* species
- *Cirsium* species
- *Coreopsis* species
- *Digitalis* species
- *Echinacea* species
- *Helenium* species
- *Lunaria annuua*
- *Miscanthus* species
- *Nigella* species
- *Pennisetum* species
- *Phlox* species
- *Rudbeckia* species
- *Stipa* species

A single oak tree can support up to a million organisms. Old trees are particularly valuable for other living organisms, especially when they contain cracks and holes and fissures. Bats and birds like to nest in tree trunks, and insects appreciate the decomposing wood.

(top left) The abundant berries on crab apple trees tempt birds in autumn.

(top right) Honeysuckle provides nectar for bumblebees, butterflies, and moths, including the hummingbird hawk moth.

(bottom left) As autumn approaches, bullfinches, warblers, and thrushes enjoy the honeysuckle berries.

(bottom right) Birds often eat the brightest coloured berries and hips first, so if you want to enjoy the bright berries for a while before they get eaten, try the paler berries of *Sorbus cashmeriana*.

feed successfully, remember to provide a separate source of food for the larger birds as well.

Water and nesting

Birds need water throughout the year to drink and to bathe in. For seed-eating birds, this water is even more essential since their food is very dry. You can make your own birdbath from a shallow dish or an upturned dustbin lid sunk into the ground but give the position of your birdbath careful thought. Birds need clear visibility so that they can keep an eye out for predators, and nearby shrubs for a quick hide-away.

You can also invite birds into your garden by providing nesting boxes. Bird boxes have been designed as a substitute for a tree hole and are quickly colonized by garden birds. The type of birds you attract to nest in your garden depends largely on the type of nesting box you choose. Bird boxes with small holes are popular with blue tits, sparrows, and nuthatches, while robins and wrens tend to prefer open-fronted boxes. Boxes with larger holes make an excellent home for great spotted woodpeckers and starlings.

To make sure your nesting box is out of the reach of cats, site it at least 2 m (6.5 ft) up a tree, fence, or wall. To prevent the nest box from overheating in hot weather, face it north or east. This avoids strong sunlight as well as the wettest winds.

Bees

Bees are important for a healthy garden; they're vital for pollinating plants, and contrary to popular opinion most bees are *not* aggressive. Interestingly, male bees can't sting at all, and female bees sting only when scared or provoked. Bees are curious creatures, always on the hunt for food, so if they do come near you, don't flap your hands about or shriek with hysteria; either keep still or move slowly into the shade—they will soon discover you are not a source of food and will move on to a nearby plant or flower.

Our bee species fall into three categories: social bees, which live in hives and produce honey; cuckoo bees, which kill the young in a hive and replace them with their own eggs; and solitary bees, which nest in holes either in wood or the ground. Our bee population, particularly

GREEN TIP **Avoid disturbing nesting birds by delaying spring and/or summer pruning and hedge cutting until late summer when young birds have fledged.**

Plants for nesting birds

- *Betula* species
- *Crateagus* species
- *Fagus* species
- *Ilex* species
- *Pinus* species
- *Quercus* species
- *Sambucus* species
- *Vitis* species

the solitary bees, is disappearing at a worrying rate because of lack of nesting sites and food.

According to the British Beekeepers' Association, in the United Kingdom about seventy crops depend on or benefit from visits by bees. In addition, bees pollinate the flowers of many plants that become part of the feed of farm animals. The economic value of honeybees and bumblebees as pollinators of commercially grown insect-pollinated crops in the United Kingdom has been estimated at more than £200 million per year.

Bee-friendly planting

A garden doesn't have to be a disheveled collection of wildflowers in order to attract bees; it doesn't have to wear its heart on its sleeve. Bee-friendly gardens can range from a traditional cottage garden through formal Italianate to the clean lines of a contemporary urban scheme, as long as they are planted with the right choice of flowers.

To encourage bees to make a home in your garden, you need to provide a range of nectar and pollen throughout the year. Pollen is important for bees because it contains proteins and fats. Nectar contains sugars and is the main energy source for bees. You may have noticed how bees flock to summer-flowering border perennials such as echinops and lavender, but since bees need a constant source of food, it is worth thinking about how we can extend the flowering season.

Crocuses are a key plant choice for the bee-friendly garden; they provide essential food for the first bees to emerge in early spring and look wonderful naturalized at the base of a tree. For later in the spring, try to include apple, foxgloves, and pyracantha. By the time summer arrives, there will be plenty of choices, but stick to these principles: Choose old-fashioned varieties over modern hybrids, as these provide the most nectar. Similarly, choose single-flowered plants rather than the more intensively bred doubles, which bees usually avoid. Anything from the rose family, including pyracantha and apple blossom, is a good bet (just go for old-fashioned, single, or species roses) as are daisy-shaped flowers, spires, and herbs with small flowers.

Some gardeners believe bees favour blue-flowering plants, so plant blue flowers such as borage in your vegetable garden to attract bees. Another good trick is to plant in blocks or drifts. As you can imagine, it is much easier to spot a good patch of food when it is grown in large

It is estimated that a third of everything we eat depends on honeybee pollination, which suggests that in 2010 bees contributed some £26 billion (roughly $38 billion) to the global economy.

(top left) Providing large quantities of pollen is important throughout the year. Good sources of summer pollen include *Philadelphus*, *Geranium*, and *Escallonia*.

(bottom left) If you see a swarm, contact the local authority or the police, and they will contact a local beekeeper to collect the swarm. Just leave them alone and wait for a competent beekeeper to arrive. Garden Collection/Jane Taylor

(top right) Buying local honey helps local beekeepers cover the costs of protecting bees.

(bottom right) Find space for a beehive—contact your local beekeeping association and they can find a beekeeper in need of a site.

GREEN TIP **Choose original species of flowering plants where possible, as these provide more nectar than hybrids.**

Butterflies and Moths

Butterflies and moths will visit any garden, large or small, if they can feed on suitable nectar plants. Important pollinators and an important food source for bats and birds, these insects are an essential part of our ecosystem. But aren't moths considered pests? While it is true that some moths, such as the clothing moth, are regarded as pests, there are plenty of moths that we really do want to encourage as garden pollinators—moths such as the hummingbird moth. We need to give these much maligned moths as much of the credit as their showier cousins.

Just like bees, butterflies prefer clumps of plants growing in a sunny, sheltered spot. When planning your butterfly garden, try to include a range of nectar plants throughout the season and remember to include plenty of host plants for the caterpillars. I often find that it's best to tuck the caterpillar host plants away in a part of the garden you don't visit too often. That way, your borders won't suffer from being munched as the caterpillars grow and build up strength. Common nettles are some of the best host plants (and also can be used to make an excellent compost tea).

Butterflies start to come out of hibernation in the spring, and native wildflowers such as primroses and violas are all good nectar providers. There are an abundance of beautiful summer flowers to choose from, such as *Veronicastrum virginicum*, *Centranthus ruber*, and cosmos. Autumn flowers such as sedum and aster, with their densely packed flower heads, provide essential nectar to help butterflies build up their winter reserves.

Other Beneficial Insects

Other beneficial insects that you can attract to your garden include ladybirds (ladybugs), lacewings, and hoverflies. These natural predators will take care of cleaning up pests that might visit your garden.

Ladybirds (ladybugs)

One of our most voracious aphid predators, and a welcome sight in any garden, the ladybird is easy to recognize by its colourful markings. Predatory ladybirds feed on aphid larvae and adult aphids (greenfly), as well as scale insects, mealybugs, and whiteflies. They are so successful at this job that some species of predatory ladybird are bred for commercial pest control.

Ladybirds have few predators of their own. Their bright colours and striking markings are a warning that they are toxic to many predators. When attacked or alarmed, ladybirds release a foul-smelling yellow fluid (reflex blood) packed full of bitter-tasting chemicals, so if you find a ladybird inside the house or shed, be gentle as you release it outside.

Most species of ladybirds hibernate throughout the winter. Among their favourite places to shelter are the leaf rosettes of perennials and other low-growing plants, so they will appreciate it if you delay cutting back all of your borders until spring. Where this is not possible, consider providing an artificial ladybird habitat for these exceptional natural predators.

UNWANTED: THE HARLEQUIN LADYBIRD

The harlequin ladybird (*Harmonia axyridis*), also known as the multicoloured Asian ladybird in Europe and the Japanese ladybug in North America, was introduced into North America in 1988 for the biological control of aphids. This invasive predator has since spread to Europe and is damaging the native ladybird population. The appearance of the harlequin ladybird varies, and it can be hard to distinguish from native ladybirds, but it is considerably larger (7 to 8 mm long compared to less than 5 mm, or about a third of an inch compared to a fifth of an inch) and more aggressive. It is easier to distinguish the harlequin larvae, as these are twice the size of the common seven-spot ladybird larvae.

One of the reasons for so much concern about the harlequin ladybird is that it is such an effective aphid predator. It eats all the aphids our native ladybirds rely on for food, and when aphids are scarce, it consumes other prey including ladybird eggs, larvae, and pupae, butterfly and moth eggs, and caterpillars. It has even been known to bite humans when hungry and is regarded as a household pest in many parts of the United States.

Harlequin ladybirds can damage fruit crops as they bulk up for winter. They are causing particular problems in vineyards, as their defensive chemicals can contaminate the wine. In addition, harlequin ladybirds have a much longer reproductive period than native ladybirds and are spreading fast.

Not all ladybirds are carnivorous predators. Some ladybirds feed on mildew and microscopic fungi, helping to control infection.

Top twenty plants to attract beneficial insects

- *Achillea millefolium*
- *Anethum graveolens*
- *Anthemis tinctoria*
- *Borago officinalis*
- *Calendula officinalis*
- *Coriandrum sativum*
- *Cosmos* species
- *Crataegus* species
- *Echinacea* species
- *Escholzia californica*
- *Foeniculum vulgare* and *F. vulgare* 'Purpurea'
- *Iberis umbellata*
- *Lavandula* species
- *Phacelia tanacelifolia*
- *Salix* species
- *Salvia* species
- *Sambucus nigra*
- *Tanacetum vulgare*
- *Thymus* species
- *Verbena* species

Researchers are working to discover how native enemies can be used to control the harlequin invasion. One of the most promising ideas is using a sexually transmitted mite that makes some ladybirds infertile. Other control options being considered are fungal disease, male-killing bacteria, a parasitic wasp, and two species of parasitic fly.

Lacewings

Lacewings are another natural predator worth supporting in your garden. Although the adults feed only on nectar and pollen, their larvae are important aphid and small insect predators and have been reported to eat between 100 and 600 aphids each. You can support lacewings in your garden by providing suitable nectar plants for the mating adults and by providing a cool, dry spot for them to overwinter, such as a garden shed or artificial lacewing habitat. Lacewings are also available commercially.

Hoverflies

Hoverflies are another useful aphid predator. Although their brightly coloured markings make these insects look a bit like bees or wasps, they are in fact true flies and do not sting. Hoverflies particularly like umbilifers such as cow parsley and fennel.

(top left) Autumn flowers such as asters provide nectar that helps butterflies build up their winter reserves.

(top right) Don't forget to provide food for the caterpillars, too, or all your efforts may be in vain. Common nettles are an excellent host plant and can often be tucked away in a quiet corner of the garden where a few munched holes will go unnoticed.

(bottom left) Buddleja is an excellent source of late summer nectar for butterflies.

(bottom right) The hundreds of tiny flowers that make up the flat head of autumn sedums supply essential nectar for the winter.

(top) This artificial habitat provides a warm, dry shelter for overwintering ladybirds and other small insects. Garden Collection/Neil Sutherland

(right) Fennel produces attractive yellow blooms that attract hoverflies, which prey on aphids.

(next page top) Yarrow will attract all sorts of beneficial insects to your garden—including lacewings, ladybirds, and hoverflies—but it may struggle to return reliably each year unless your soil is free-draining.

(next page bottom) Calendula is a traditional companion plant used to attract beneficial insects that will keep garden pests at bay.

Plants for butterflies

‡ long-flowering plants

SPRING
- *Cornus* species
- *Primula veris*
- *Primula vulgaris*
- *Ribes* species
- *Salix caprea*
- *Viola riviniana*

EARLY SUMMER
- *Allium schoenoprasum*
- *Borago officinalis*
- *Cornus* species
- *Cosmos* species
- *Cytisus scoparius*
- *Calendula officinalis*
- *Centaurea cyanus*
- *Centranthus ruber*
- *Cirsium* species ‡
- *Deschampsia cespitosa* ‡
- *Dianthus* species, especially *D. barbatus*
- *Echinops* species ‡
- *Eryngium* species ‡
- *Erysimum cheiri*
- *Escallonia* species ‡
- *Helianthemum*
- *Hemerocallis* species
- *Hesperis matronalis*
- *Ilex aquifolium*
- *Lavandula* species
- *Lobularia maritima*
- *Lonicera periclymenum*
- *Lunaria annua*

- *Malva* species
- *Mentha* species
- *Origanum* species ‡
- *Phlox* species ‡
- *Prunus spinosa*
- *Rosa canina*
- *Salvia* species
- *Sanguisorba minor*
- *Syringa* species
- *Tagetes erecta* and *T. patula*
- *Thymus* species ‡
- *Trifolium* species
- *Verbena* species ‡
- *Viola* species ‡

LATE SUMMER
- *Achillea* species
- *Agastache* species
- *Buddleja* species
- *Ceratostigma* species ‡
- *Cirsium* species ‡
- *Deschampsia cespitosa* ‡
- *Echinops* species ‡
- *Echinacea* species
- *Eryngium* species ‡
- *Escallonia* species ‡
- *Eupatorium* species
- *Festuca* species
- *Hebe* species
- *Humulus lupulus*
- *Leucanthemum* ×*superbum*
- *Lobelia* species
- *Molinia caerulea*
- *Monarda* species
- *Origanum* species ‡
- *Phlox* species ‡

- *Sesleria caerulea*
- *Thymus* species ‡
- *Trifolium* species
- *Tropaeolum majus*
- *Verbena* species ‡

AUTUMN / WINTER
- *Aster* species
- *Euonymus europaeus*
- *Sedum* species

Plants for caterpillars

- fennel
- stinging nettles
- holly
- mixed grasses
- thistle

Plants for moths

The best plants for attracting moths to your garden are those that have a strong scent at night.

- *Epilobium* species
- *Jasminum* species
- *Lonicera* species
- *Matthiola* species
- *Nicotiana* species
- *Sedum* species

11

Growing Your Own Food
and Cut Flowers

Interest in "grow your own" has seen a resurgence over recent years. With even the smallest of spaces you can enjoy fresh and tasty produce without food miles—but watch out, it's addictive! Try allocating an area of your garden to growing fruits and vegetables. If you have a limited amount of space, concentrate on growing the things you like to eat best or have most difficulty obtaining sustainably. I am a big fan of soft fruits and berries, but I also make sure to grow sugar snap peas (which always seem to be flown in from distant climes) and cut-and-come-again lettuce.

You can also grow flowers for cutting without having to set aside a special bed for them. This is more sustainable than buying them from a store, since in most cases they will have been shipped in from a different continent. Think how much fresher food and flowers can be when simply brought in from outside your kitchen door.

Start with Salad

Salad is one of the easiest things to grow in a kitchen garden and is a great place to start if you are a novice. You can choose from an overwhelming variety of leaves to grow, even in the depths of winter, with many varieties available for cropping within fourteen days of sowing. You don't need a lot of space to grow your fresh salad leaves, either; I find a couple of 60-cm (about 2-ft) window boxes are sufficient to support two people with a variety of "saladings" throughout the year.

The key to growing salad leaves on a cut-and-come-again basis is to regularly harvest the larger leaves. For the best flavour, snip them off with a pair of scissors just before eating. Regular harvesting encourages the smaller leaves to grow, and within a few days you will have another crop. If you make successional sowings of seeds every three to four weeks, you will have a constant supply of salad throughout the year.

You can sow seeds indoors in a propagator throughout the winter, but from late spring on you should be able to sow seeds directly into pots, window boxes, and raised beds outside.

You would be surprised how much fresh produce you can grow in the smallest of spaces. Cut-and-come-again salad is one of the easiest crops to start with.

(top left) Rocket (arugula) can be grown year-round. Sow salad rocket from midautumn to late spring, then wild rocket until midautumn.

(top right) Buckler-leaved sorrel has tasty green leaves with a hint of apple.

(bottom left) Winter salad choices are more limited, but winter purslane can be relied upon when grown under a cloche.

(bottom right) Don't limit yourself to traditional salad leaves; try harvesting the leaves of 'Bull's Blood' beetroot for a splash of colour in your salad.

(above) Never walk on your raised beds or you will damage the soil structure. When designing your vegetable garden, make sure you can comfortably reach all parts of the raised bed from the paths. Jane Sebire (designer Chris Beardshaw)

(top right) Raised beds are simple to construct. Stakes at the corners reinforce the 90 degree angle but also help to secure the frame into the ground. Jane Sebire (designer Alison Mundie at RHS Garden Harlow Carr, North Yorkshire)

(bottom right) Close plant spacing makes a living mulch that shades roots and reduces evaporation losses.

(above) Woven willow or hazel (hazelnut) is a classic choice for raised vegetable beds. Jane Sebire

(left) Many garden retailers now offer a fabric planter with woven surround that can be packed flat when not in use. Home Allotment Willow Planters/Burgon and Ball

and 3.8 cm thick) are ideal. If you are buying new wood, you can go as small as 15 cm (6 in) wide and 2.5 cm (1 in) thick. Look out for the FSC or PEFC quality standard and avoid preservatives and treated wood (this includes pressure-treated timber). Most raised beds are just 22 cm high (the width of a scaffold board). Some are simply braced at the corners and laid on top of the ground, while others incorporate stakes at each corner to brace the structure and secure it to the ground.

Once your raised bed has been built, all you need to do is fill it with spare garden soil or homemade compost. If you are concerned about the nutrient levels in your soil, make your first crop a green manure—don't buy in compost unless you have exhausted all your other options.

Crop Rotation

Growing the same crop in the same spot year after year can cause a build-up of pests and soil disease, and can severely diminish available nutrients. A better system is to move your crops around the growing area. Crop rotation is a traditional idea that is still useful for gardeners today. It was originally practiced as a way of maintaining soil fertility, alternating crops that deplete the soil's minerals with crops that actually improve the soil and add nutrients. Crop rotation also helps to protect your crops from pests and disease, such as club root, a fungal disease that devastates plants in the cabbage family (but is harmless for other vegetables). If you have four beds in your vegetable plot and grow your cabbage in bed 1 the first year, bed 2 the second year, and so on, by the time you plant your cabbage in bed 1 again (in year 5), the fungal spores will have disappeared and your cabbage will be safe.

Crop rotation relies on growing plants in the same family together. For example, members of the carrot family, including carrot, celeriac, fennel, parsley, and parsnips, would all be grown together. There are nine vegetable families in total: beetroot, cabbage, carrot (including celery), daisy (lettuce and endive), marrow (courgettes), onion, pea and bean, potato, and a final miscellaneous group (sweet corn). Here is one way to group the families into beds:

BED 1: POTATOES AND ONIONS
New potatoes and tomatoes followed by leeks for winter

BED 2: PEAS AND BEANS, MARROW

> Peas, broad beans, French beans, runner beans, and courgettes (zucchini)

BED 3: CABBAGE

> Broccoli, kale, mustard, radish, cabbage

BED 4: ROOTS, ONIONS, LETTUCE

> Turnips, beetroots, parsnips, onions, garlic, shallots, carrots
> Salad leaves, spinach, chard, lettuce, parsley, sweet corn, celery

You can choose from lots of different systems of crop rotation, but the simplest strategy is to work on a three- or four-year crop rotation such as the one described here.

A Cut-Flower Garden

With retail sales of over £2billion, the British cut-flower market is comparable in size to the music industry, yet nearly 90 percent of these flowers are imported from outside the United Kingdom. In the United States a similar story unfolds: Americans spend more than $6 billion a year on cut flowers, 78 percent of which are imported.

Buy local

Supermarkets and florists have been listening to customer demand and have improved their sourcing and labeling of locally grown flowers. In the United Kingdom, most supermarkets now offer prominently labeled British-grown flowers, and Costco in the United States recently committed to stocking Rainforest Alliance Certified roses. The standards developed by the Rainforest Alliance "protect ecosystems and wildlife habitats, conserve water and soil, promote decent and safe working conditions, and ensure that the farms are good neighbors to rural communities and wildlands."

Grow your own bouquets

There is no denying that cut flowers are a wonderful luxury, but did you know how easy it is to grow flowers for cutting in your own garden? When designing planting schemes for gardens, I like to include a bal-

GREEN TIP Look for the VeriFlora label on fresh-cut flowers and potted plants in the United States and Canada to know that you are buying products that meet North America's most comprehensive sustainability certification standard.

(right) At Country Roses near Colchester, Danae and Robin Duthy grow hybrid tea, floribunda, and bush roses for cutting.

(bottom left) Sweet peas will offer armfuls of scented flowers throughout the summer. Remember to keep harvesting them or they will stop producing new flowers.

(bottom right) Peonies will wilt very quickly in a sunny garden. I like to cut mine just as the buds are opening, as they last much longer in a vase on my desk.

(next page) Cosmos are among my favourite flowers for cutting and are easy to grow from seed.

Favourite flowers for cutting

- *Cosmos* species (quick to grow from seed)
- *Dianthus barbatus* (drought tolerant)
- *Eryngium* species (drought tolerant and good for wildlife)
- *Hesperis matronalis* (good for wildlife)
- *Lathyrus* species
- *Narcissus* 'Thalia', *N. poeticus*, *N.* 'Jenny'
- *Papaver nudicaule*, *P. somniferum* (good for wildlife and to grow from seed)
- *Rosa* 'Felicia', *R.* 'Iceberg', *R.* 'New Dawn', *R.* 'Nuits de Young', *R.* 'Graham Thomas'
- *Rosa moyesii* 'Geranium', *R. glauca*, *R. mulliganii* (hips are good for birds)

ance of foliage and flowers that work just as well in the vase as they do in the border. If space is limited, I tend to concentrate on roses, tulips, and foliage plants that can be used to bulk up shop-bought stems.

Unless you have room for a dedicated cutting garden, you will need to try getting a balance of flowers to leave in the garden and flowers to cut for the house. You don't want to end up with bare borders. With some plants this is easy; peonies and irises, for example, contribute strong foliage and elegant buds to a planting scheme but the delicate flowers can quickly go over in a day or two of baking sunshine. I often cut these just as the flowers are coming out, for they last much longer inside in a vase. With a number of other perennials (such as echinops and eryngium), you can gather flowers for the house and prune to stagger flowering time both at the same time. Cut back the front half of a large clump, or the back clumps where the plant is repeated. You'll have lovely flowers to bring inside and enjoy, as well as delaying the flowering of the cut perennials, which will extend the flowering season in the garden.

Overall, I like to take no more than a third of flowering plants for the house. Remember, when taking flowers for cutting, prune the stems back to a vigorous shooting bud, and it will produce lots of new flowering shoots. Cutting in this way will make many of your garden plants (especially the roses) even more floriferous.

A GARDEN FOR CUTTING IN NOTTINGHAM

In a garden I designed in Nottingham, more half of the plants on the plant list provide excellent material for cutting. In the yellow garden, *Rosa* 'Canary Bird' starts flowering in early spring, followed by *Rosa* 'Graham Thomas' and *Rosa* 'Gloire de Dijon' in midsummer. *Alchemilla erythropoda* (less invasive than the more common *Alchemilla mollis*) provides sprays of early filler material and makes a lovely bouquet in combination with white roses and pale pink astrantias.

12

Maintaining the
Greener Garden

A low-maintenance garden is top of the list for most garden owners, but no garden is entirely maintenance free. There will always be storm cleanup, plants that flop over, weeds, pests, and areas that need mowing. How you manage these challenges and tasks will affect your garden's green credentials just as much as the decisions you made as you laid out your garden's hard landscaping and planting areas. Garden maintenance can be made easier and greener, avoiding the need for chemical pesticides and polluting equipment, through some simple pruning and gardening tricks.

Pruning for Storm Resistance

One of the best ways to lower the maintenance requirements of your garden is to use pruning techniques to adapt the shape of your favourite plants so that they will sustain less damage in a storm. You may already have noticed that shrubs are often able to withstand strong winds without being uprooted, and you can take advantage of this observation by training more-susceptible plants to grow in this fashion. Try using multi-stem trees instead of standards, so that the branches filter and slow the wind. You can also prune trees and shrubs into a pollarded or coppiced specimen for a similar effect. Many plants react well after a strong pruning, and you will find it easier to restore storm-damaged plants if they are accustomed to the discipline of being cut back hard on a regular basis.

As we have already seen, the right combination of plants can reduce garden chores and help to protect plants from the elements. Layered plantings are a great way to combine lots of plant activity in a small area and to crowd out weeds. The key to any layered planting is to make sure every one of the plants in the group has enough space for healthy growth. Lifting the crown of a shrub or tree is a very simple way to create more space for an understory of plants. Simply remove the lower limbs from the central trunk up to a height of 1 m (about 3 ft). This will retain the shape and vigour of the plant while opening up plenty of space for planting underneath.

Pollarding is a pruning technique that keeps trees and shrubs smaller than they would naturally grow. Limbs are cut back hard to the main stem and allowed to regenerate. Coppicing is a pruning technique in which the stems of a tree or shrub are periodically cut down to the ground and allowed to regenerate.

No More Staking

Few of us can devote the time required to the endless tying-in and staking of traditional herbaceous borders, but you can obtain the same look with far less effort if you adopt a few gardening tricks. Plants tend to flop and collapse for three main reasons: they are too pampered, top-heavy, or too tall.

Giving your perennials too much water or overfeeding your plants is an easy way to end up with weak, leggy, sappy plants. Instead of spoiling your plants, force them to fight a bit more for the water and nutrients they require. You will be rewarded with sturdier, slow-growing plants that are largely self-sufficient. Fuss over your plants too much and you will end up with plants that are constantly relying on you for support.

Peasticks for support

One of the best ways to prevent broken stems and collapsing plants is to use peasticks to support vulnerable plants as they grow. Peasticks are stems of birch or hazel that have been harvested in early spring with the side shoots still intact. They usually vary from 1 to 1.5 m (roughly 3 to 5 ft) in height and can be densely branched. In midspring, while your perennials are still small, push these peasticks into the ground so that they form a ring or cage around peonies, geraniums, and other problem plants. When installing your peasticks, make sure at least a third of the stem is underground, or the plant support itself might collapse. The network of branching stems will provide a natural twiggy support as the plant grows, and by the time your border comes into flower, these peasticks will be hidden by foliage.

Plants that support themselves

When planning the planting for your garden, you can cut down your workload by choosing plants that are self-supporting. Avoid top-heavy perennials with large individual flowers or wide dense flower heads and go for the shorter varieties with smaller flowers. The biggest flops in the border tend to be hybrids that have been bred with oversized or double blooms. Tinkering with plants in this way makes them unbalanced and

GREEN TIP To avoid winter frost damage, leave your roses unpruned until all danger of frost has passed. If you want to cut your roses back before spring (to keep the garden tidy), leave the stems a good 7 to 12 cm (3 to 5 in) longer than normal. This will allow you to prune away any frost damage in the spring without giving your roses too severe a haircut.

GREEN TIP Instead of hybrid delphiniums, consider the spires of *Veronicastrum viginicum*, *Eremurus*, or *Cimicifuga*, which are less prone to flop.

Cut back the foliage and stems of summer-flowering perennials by a third in late spring or early summer to encourage sturdy, compact plants.

unable to support themselves. If you want to avoid spending your time in the garden staking your perennials, choose plants that are closer to the species.

Some plants are naturally tall. Others grow tall trying to reach the light. A sun-loving perennial will grow tall and leggy in the shade as it struggles to find enough light. Overcrowded borders, with many plants competing for light and space, can result in tall, spindly specimens. Think carefully about each plant's requirements when designing a planting plan. Will there be enough light? How quickly does it grow in relation to its neighbours? Is there enough room to mature?

The Chelsea chop

Many of the tallest perennials in the border can be converted into self-supporting plants with a timely bit of summer pruning. The Chelsea chop is the most famous pruning technique for herbaceous perennials. Around the time of the Royal Horticultural Society Chelsea Flower Show, in late spring, the foliage and stems of summer-flowering perennials are cut back by a third to encourage a dense, branching perennial that distributes its weight more evenly.

Cutting back plants in early summer can transform a sprawling, floppy perennial into a sturdy, compact plant. Sedums are a spectacular example of how this simple intervention works, and I have found you can get away with cutting them back as late as July without losing the autumn flowers.

Once you have got the hang of the principle, you can use this technique to control the size of perennials in the border, reduce the need to stake, produce more flowers, and even stagger or delay the flowering of a plant within your borders. The closer you cut back a perennial to the flowering time, the less it will regrow and the more you will delay eventual flowering. You can even take this opportunity to prune your perennials into a dome to stagger the height of your flowers.

Weed Management

The key to dealing with weeds is (where possible) to tackle them while they are small. You will save yourself a lot of time and trouble if you learn how to spot weeds when they are just sprouting, and especially if you can catch them before they set seed. My mother always told me

(top left) Cutting back perennials can prevent the need to stake a plant and will also result in more flowers.

(top right) *Verbena bonariensis* is a very sturdy plant despite its height and airy open structure—in fact, it is so strong that it can often be found supporting other collapsed perennials in the border.

(bottom left) *Eupatorium* (Joe Pye weed) has strong stalks and should never require staking although it will perform noticeably better if given an extra bucket of water or two during the growing season.

(bottom right) Peasticks (stems of birch or hazel harvested in early spring) can be used to support problem plants such as peonies and geraniums.

GREEN TIP **Tackle weeds while they are small and use the least harmful methods—hoeing, hand weeding, light exclusion, flaming—before even considering chemicals.**

that weeds are just plants that are in the wrong place, but now I've realized that more than that, weeds are plants that are just a bit too successful.

Weeds can be useful to the gardener. They act like a green manure, preventing soil erosion and keeping the soil structure in place. Nettles are an excellent sign that a soil is fertile, and they make an outstanding liquid feed; they just tend to grow much more quickly than other plants so can outcompete them for light and nutrients. Aggressive plants such as mint and *Centranthus ruber* can soon take over a garden if you don't keep them in check, while some gardeners find them desirable.

Hoeing

Hoes are the first line of attack in the fight to control weeds, perfect for bumping off baby weed seedlings just as they take their first steps. For the best results, choose a sunny day and a sharp hoe. Simply push the blade along the bed just under the surface of the soil, and the decapitated seedlings will quickly shrivel in the sun.

Hand weeding

Once weeds get too big to dispatch with your hoe, you will have to start weeding by hand. Some shallow-rooting weeds can simply be pulled gently, especially if there is plenty of moisture in the soil. Others, such as dandelions or dock (with their long taproots), will need a bit of help from a hand fork, daisy grubber, or dandelion weeder.

Light exclusion

Light exclusion kills weeds by blocking out all the light with an impermeable material like cardboard or geotextile. Many gardeners choose to use a thick sheet of polythene or black plastic, but I prefer to use two or three layers of cardboard (overlapping so there are no gaps for the light to get through). I water this thoroughly so that it doesn't blow away in a sudden gust of wind and then cover it with mulch. Destroying weeds by light exclusion takes patience. Some annual weeds will die off in a matter of months, but tough perennial weeds may take years to defeat.

Horticultural vinegar

Some gardeners use horticultural vinegar to tackle their weed problem. This eco-friendly vinegar has a higher concentration of acetic acid than the malt vinegar you might expect to find in your kitchen, but it is a nonselective herbicide so it may damage the plants you want to keep as well as the weeds you want to remove. I'm not convinced that horticultural vinegars are all that useful in the greener garden, and I'm going to stick to hand weeding and my trusty hoe.

Flaming

Organic standards allow flame weeding, which uses a high-temperature flame to destroy the internal cell structure of plants. Rather than setting fire to them, the heat causes weeds to wither and die. Flame weeders are particularly useful for weeding cracks in paving, but they use disposable gas canisters so they are not particularly high on the sustainability scale.

Pest Management with Chemicals

When used for their correct purpose and in a responsible manner, chemical pesticides can have a role in the garden—but think carefully before you reach for the chemicals, as you may do more harm than good. Chemicals are not the only or best way of controlling pests and diseases. Most problems can be avoided by good gardening practice such as choosing the right plant for the site, rotating crops, and hand-picking pests and diseased leaves.

One of the main problems with garden chemicals is that most are not selective and may kill the beneficial insects as well as the target. When the original pest returns, there will be no natural enemy to fight against it, so it will return in even greater numbers. Regular use can lead to the development of resistance.

It must be remembered that pesticides are poisons—this is how they work—so should be used only as a last resort. If a plant regularly experiences problems with pest or disease, you are probably trying to grow it in less-than-ideal conditions. Replace it with something more appropriate that will not be stressed and vulnerable, and you will have solved the problem without resorting to chemicals.

Next time you are considering using chemicals in the garden, have a think about whether they are really necessary. Check the problem is not caused by a cold snap or mineral deficiencies, in which case chemicals have no hope of helping the situation. Next consider how serious

Vineyard owners in the Napa Valley of California are using lambs to mow the vineyards. At present, sheep are mainly used in the winter months or while the grapes are still bitter and juvenile. In other parts of the United States, researchers are using aversion therapy to train sheep not to eat the grapes in vineyards, which could make this a viable option year-round.

GREEN TIP **Replace plants that regularly experience problems with something more comfortable with the conditions your garden naturally provides.**

Use a combination of strategies—nematodes, handpicking and traps, barriers, slug pellets, unappealing plants—to stop slugs and snails.

the problem is; minor damage can and should be tolerated. In the rare instance where you decide chemicals really are the most sensible solution, make sure you apply them at the right stage of the life cycle—be it of the plant or pest. Do not apply chemicals on a windy day or if rain is expected, or you will contaminate other plants and even the water cycle.

Pest Management—Slugs and Snails

Slugs and snails are a fierce adversary for the gardener. Feeding mainly at night, they can chomp their way through all your lush-leaved plants, leaving a trail of devastation in their wake. More home remedies exist for dealing with slugs than for any other garden foe, which suggests what tricky little blighters they are. A recent trial by the BBC Gardeners World Team demonstrated that nothing stops slugs and snails entirely but that a combination of attack strategies, and a resignation that some damage is inevitable, can keep these terrors under control.

Nematodes

The best way to start your campaign against these slimy foes is with a regular application of nematodes. The microscopic nematode *Phasmarhabditis hermaphrodita* is a native species found in the soil throughout the United Kingdom. (Although investigations into its possible use in the United States are ongoing, there is currently no U.S. equivalent.) U.K. residents can buy extra nematodes under the brand name Nemaslug; the nematodes come in a pack of moist clay that can be mixed with water and applied to the soil with a watering can. One application of this nematode will control your slug population for up to six weeks, so regular applications between March and October will ensure the best chance of success. Research has shown that nematodes are most effective against small and soil-dwelling slugs that are difficult to control by other methods, but they are only effective when the soil temperature reaches 5 degrees C (41 degrees F) or more.

Handpicking and traps

Another popular approach is to go out into the garden after dark with a torch (flashlight) or headlamp and pick them off by hand. Many gardeners choose to snip their slugs in half with a pair of scissors, although you can crush them or give them to the birds to eat. Some gardeners swear by slug traps, the most famous of which is the beer trap. When burying your beer trap in the ground, always try to leave at least 2 cm (1 in) protruding above soil level so that you don't trap innocent bugs and beetles, too. Other traps lure slugs in with the promise of a moist, dark shelter. A few spare roofing tiles or half grapefruit skins seem to appeal, and you can turn them over every few days and collect all the slugs.

Barriers

Many gardeners choose to use physical barriers to keep slugs away from their favourite plants. A number of these—such as wood chips, eggshells, seashells, and gravel—rely on a sharp, coarse texture to discourage slugs. Others, like bran or comfrey rings, offer another source of food so that the slug is too full to eat the most precious plants. Wool pellets, made from extruded, reclaimed wool, have been successfully tested at the Royal Horticultural Society garden Harlow Carr. These wool pellets form a biodegradable blanket around the plant that irritates the nerve endings of the slugs when they try to cross. The wool also acts as a soil conditioner and mulch. Copper rings, copper impregnated mats, and copper pot feet give a natural electric charge that keeps all but the most sadistic slugs away, but a glass or bottle cloche is probably the most foolproof method.

Sacrificial plants

If you have resigned yourself to the fact that some damage will be inevitable, you could take a different line of attack and allow some of your less precious plants to get eaten. Tasty green lettuces are a real distraction for slugs and will keep your favourite plants safe from attack.

Predators on patrol

Slugs are a tasty treat for all sorts of birds, including thrushes, robins, and blackbirds, so encourage them to make a home in your garden by providing nesting boxes and a source of water. You may choose to keep ducks or hens to keep the slug population down—but they might also eat your seedlings, so a better choice might be to attract frogs, toads, and hedgehogs to feast upon your slugs by providing a variety of wildlife habitats.

(top left) To keep slugs off, some gardeners swear by a ring of used coffee grounds. Others prefer a by-product of rooibos tea. Whichever method you prefer, you will have the best chance of success with a range of different approaches.

(top right) The thick, waxy leaves of bergenia are tough enough to deter even the hungriest slug.

(bottom left) Aromatic plants, such as this purple sage, often escape a slug rampage unmolested. It seems the slugs are put off by the strong scent.

(bottom right) Lady's mantle is a popular choice for the slug-infested garden, perhaps because of its hairy leaves.

Slug pellets

Traditionally, slug baits have been made of metaldehyde, a chemical that is toxic to the nervous system. Mataldehyde can also affect birds, dogs, and even horses, causing death from respiratory and liver failure, so it is best avoided at all costs. A better choice is to use a slug pellet based on iron phosphate. This new type of slug pellet has been approved for organic gardening and targets only slugs and snails. Birds and other animals are said to suffer no adverse affects from eating these pellets, and uneaten pellets will break down into phosphate and iron to be taken up as plant nutrients. Iron phosphate is an abundant mineral so is a pretty sustainable choice.

Aromatics and other unappealing plants

If you have a particular problem with slugs in your garden, it can be worth avoiding vulnerable plants such as hostas and delphiniums, which offer gourmet dining for slugs and snails. Slugs tend to leave plants with a strong scent alone, so aromatics such as lavender, rosemary, catmint, and fennel often escape unharmed. Slugs also show a distaste for plants with a waxy finish, such as bergenia; plants with a sour taste, such as the sap-filled euphorbia; and hairy plants such as yarrow, lady's mantle (*Alchemilla mollis*), and verbascum.

Pest Management—Aphids

Aphids are a common garden pest. They suck the sap from plants, causing them to wilt and die, and can spread infection as they move about the garden. You don't have to resort to chemical warfare to get rid of these pests. There are plenty of greener options to consider.

Blast of water

One of the simplest ways to tackle an infestation of aphids is to use water pressure to blast them off their host plant, although this method has several potential problems. First, a high-pressure spray can damage delicate plants; second, as water becomes an increasingly rare commodity in the garden, this method can be seen as a waste of water; and third, damp conditions cause fungal infections to spread. You can handpick aphids and infested leaves off the plants and drop them into a bucket of soapy water (very time consuming), or you can spray the infested areas of the plant with an insecticidal soap spray.

GREEN TIP Grow hostas in poor, sandy soil if you want to avoid slug attack. Although hostas are normally recommended for rich clay soils, they grow so lush there they are almost always destined for failure. In a sandy soil, the leaves stay compact and can often avoid attack.

Companion planting is a great way to manage pests such as aphids without resorting to chemicals. The idea is similar to that of plant guilds and beneficial plant associations in that communities of plants support one another, aiding pollination and keeping pest numbers down. Companion plants work in a number of ways:

* attracting pollinators for fruits and vegetables

* confusing pests by masking the scent of the plants

* attracting predatory insects to prey on pests

* providing support, shade, or shelter for other plants

* camouflaging the plants that pests search for by sight

* acting as sacrificial plants so that the main crops are not eaten

Common companion plantings include underplanting roses with nepeta or lavender to deter aphids, and planting French marigolds alongside tomatoes. Here are some other noteworthy companion plants:

Alliums are a large group of plants including garlic, onions, leeks, and chives, classically planted with carrots. The strong scent of the alliums effectively wards off carrot fly, while the smell of the carrots seems to be very effective at deterring onion fly: a match made in heaven. Alliums are also claimed to deter slugs and aphids, although the jury is still out.

Borage is a frost-hardy annual with hairy leaves and pretty blue flowers. Bees, butterflies, and other pollinators seem to love this plant, and flock to feast upon its nectar. Borage is said to improve the flavour of strawberries if planted nearby, and its young leaves and flowers can be added to salads.

Marigolds are some of the most useful companion plants around. *Calendula officinalis* is a frost-hardy annual that repels whitefly, aphids, and carrot fly, protecting everything from tomatoes to beans. Adored by slugs, they also make an excellent sacrificial plant, and if that wasn't already enough, they attract a whole range of aphid predators including hoverflies, lacewings, and ladybirds.

Mint deters a whole range of pests with its strongly scented leaves—but grow it in a pot or this hardy perennial will take over your garden. For a bit of variety, try the rust-resistant *Mentha spicata* var. *crispa* 'Moroccan', which is great with salads and potatoes—and perfect for fresh mint tea.

Nasturtiums are often used as a sacrificial plant to protect French beans, runner beans, and brassicas from pest damage. The pretty sunny flowers of *Tropaleum majus* help to attract the beneficial insects that prey on aphids, while providing a splash of colour that lasts throughout the summer. Available as annual bedding or climbing plants, they are also delicious in salads.

(top left) Mint deters a whole range of pests with its strongly scented leaves.

(top right) Marigolds are some of the most useful companion plants around. *Calendula officinalis* is a frost-hardy annual that repels whitefly, aphids and carrot fly, protecting everything from tomatoes to beans. Don't get too attached to your marigolds, though, as it seems slugs love them, too.

(bottom left) Alliums are a large group of plants including garlic, onions, leeks, and chives. Their strong scent makes them an effective partner to carrots as they seem to keep pesky carrot flies at bay.

(bottom right) Underplanting roses with allium can deter aphids.

Natural predators

A far better choice is to encourage natural predators by providing suitable food and wildlife habitats. Hoverflies, lacewings, and ladybirds are all effective aphid predators. Attract them to your garden by growing the plants and flowers they love (listed in chapter 10). Blue tits are a less well known aphid predator and will happily eat aphid eggs over the winter months. Attract them to your worst affected plants (such as fruit trees and roses) by hanging fat balls in strategic parts of the garden.

Pest Management—Other Pests

Wasps, termites, and small animals may also threaten the peace and health of your garden, but there are natural methods for dealing with all of these.

Wasps

Wasps tend to be thought of as a garden pest, but since they pollinate our garden plants and prey on aphids we should perhaps reclassify them as beneficial insects. Wasps cause the most annoyance at mealtimes, when they buzz about your plate and drink in their search for food. A traditional wasp trap—usually consisting of a glass jar with an opening in the bottom and a sealed top that lures wasps in with a sweet, sticky bait—works by attracting and then trapping and killing wasps. Wasp traps can look quite elegant hung from the branches of an apple orchard, but they can be messy and are a pain to clean.

A far better solution is to use a fake wasps' nest, such as the Waspinator from Contech Enterprises (www.contech-inc.com/products/waspinator/), to scare wasps away from the dinner table altogether. Social wasps, such as the common wasp (*Vespula vulgaris*), are aggressive insects and will keenly defend the territory around their nests by attacking and killing interlopers. A fake wasps' nest works by tricking wasps into thinking there is an enemy nest in the area. The wasps will keep away from the enemy nest (or fake nest) for fear of their life, giving you a wasp-free area to enjoy in peace.

Insecticidal soap spray contains fatty acids that clog up the breathing apparatus of aphids, causing them to suffocate and die.

Termites

Termites can cause real problems in gardens and are especially keen on eating wooden decks and raised beds. There are two types of termites: subterranean and drywood. Subterranean termites dwell in the soil and tunnel up to the surface to find wood, while drywood termites enter wood from the air, not the ground.

With wooden decks, it can help to try and keep the wood as dry as possible to deter the subterranean termites. Keep surrounding planting from touching the deck, use saucers with any plant pots (to stop water soaking through), and direct any runoff away from the deck. For all other garden structures, a barrier is a better solution to deter subterranean termites.

Barriers using 16-grit sand can be used to surround wooden structures in contact with the ground. This sand makes a good protective shield (a bit like a moat), as it is too big for subterranean termites to burrow through. Vulnerable wood can also be clad with stainless steel caps or a special termite-proof mesh. Nematodes are also available to tackle these termites.

Drywood termites are harder to beat. Call in the professionals.

Rabbits, deer, and other mammals

Rabbits and deer can cause real problems in a garden. They strip the bark off young trees, causing them to bleed to death, and they like to eat the tender shoots and leaves of trees, shrubs, and herbaceous plants. The best solution is to fence off the entire garden, but this can be an overwhelming undertaking in larger landscapes—especially when you remember that rabbits can dig. Rabbits can also squeeze their bodies through impossibly small gaps, so any successful rabbitproof fence will need to be just as robust under the ground as it is above it. A deerproof fence will need to be even more substantial. Deer can jump even a 1.5-m (5-ft) fence and can easily flatten a fence by leaning on it.

There are no truly rabbitproof or deerproof plants. Few garden plants are granted a reprieve from these voracious feeders. Gardeners are always keen to swap tales of the plants that survived a visit from local rabbits or deer, but they very rarely tally across the country. Resistant plants vary hugely from location to location; many plant lists hail hydrangeas as deer-resistant plants, but in my experience these are

(right) Rabbits love to eat our favourite garden plants, especially the fresh new shoots. Garden Collection/Andew Parkinson FLPA

(below) Spiky barberry is one of the few plants that deer won't try to eat.

(next page top) Kniphofia is another tough, drought tolerant perennial that usually escapes the attention of rabbits and deer. In this planting it is combined with nepeta and Salvia 'Purple Rain' for an eyecatching contrast of colour and texture.

(next page bottom) Plants with tough, waxy leaves such as *Aucuba japonica*, cotoneaster, and skimmia are usually safe from hungry rabbits.

GREEN TIP **Discourage unwanted garden invaders with a solar-charged electric fence.**

some of the worst affected—all new shoots grazed right down to the ground. With so few guidelines to follow, the best advice I can give is to consult your local council (agricultural extension) for advice or concentrate on hairy, waxy, bitter, and spiky plants such as acanthus, barberry, viburnum, forsythia, and skimmia.

SCARING DEER IN KENT

In a garden I designed in Kent, the existing 1.5-m (5-ft) boundary walls were not enough to keep deer out of the garden. However, we did not want to compromise the views across the surrounding landscape by fencing them out. One option would have been to create a ha-ha or ditch outside of the boundary walls, but in this instance we found sound scarers to be an effective method of control. Studies have shown that the simultaneous use of light and the human voice is one of the most effective deer deterrents. When activated by a motion sensor, the sound scarer turns on an FM radio and a bright LED light. It sounds like a bit of a silly idea but it seems to work.

Moles, voles, and gophers

Gophers, moles, and voles can cause untold destruction to a garden, but they mean no harm. You can repel them with predator urine or solar-powered vibrations. In the wild, animals use urine to mark their territory. Animals lower down the food chain (the prey) go by this scent to know which areas to avoid for fear of becoming dinner. There are various types of predator urine on the market (both natural and synthetic). Vibrating devices emit a deep vibrating noise at a pitch inaudible to humans. It has been suggested that this causes a mole to leave your garden because it thinks there is another mole in the area. Alternatively, you can go for the traditional approach of keeping them away from your plants with wire barriers and underground fencing.

Powering Garden Maintenance

Vehicle exhaust emissions have been dramatically reduced over the last couple of decades, but it is only in the last few years that regulatory attention has turned to mobile nonroad machinery such as lawn mowers, chainsaws, and leaf blowers.

Modern gas-powered lawn mowers tend to have four-cycle (or four-stroke) engines, making them much more efficient than the older, oil-thirsty two-cycle engines, but even these modern lawn mowers produce dangerous emissions. Gas-powered garden machinery pours out smog in the form of volatile hydrocarbons, lung-poisoning particulates, and suffocating gases such as carbon monoxide and dioxide. Spilled fuel from garden machinery seeps into the ground and contaminates the water table, or it evaporates, contributing to air pollution.

Noise pollution is a further problem: how often are we distracted at work by grounds staff with noisy equipment? How often is our enjoyment of the garden ruined by a noisy lawn mower or leaf blower? So get rid of your gas-powered equipment. A far better choice is a traditional push or reel mower, or if your garden is too large to rely on a manual mower, choose equipment powered by alternative fuels.

I have yet to hear a good argument for using a leaf blower. They are noisy, they do not use a renewable source of power, and they spread dust, particulates, and disease all over the place. In many instances, leaves are best left where they fall, as they can provide a protective mulch for plantings. Leaves on the lawn can be shredded with a lawnmower and used as a winter mulch, or raked up and used to make leaf mould. On paths and driveways, they are equally easy to bag up and make into leaf mould.

Go electric

With the wealth of alternative fuel options being touted at the moment, it can be hard to determine the best choice. Electric mowers have shaken off the burden of trailing power cords, short battery life, and limited horsepower and are becoming a viable option. Previous generations of electric mowers needed nine to twenty-four hours to fully recharge, but a new generation with 36V lithium-ion batteries can fully recharge in just an hour. Electric mowers are emission-free, and if your electricity comes from a power plant that uses natural gas or a renewable such as hydropower, they are almost virtuous. Furthermore, electric mowers cut noise by half—below the levels that cause ear damage.

Solar power

For many gardeners, the most sustainable choice is solar-powered machinery. Most of these use removable batteries that are charged by the sun (rather than being charged using electricity from the grid).

GREEN TIP Get rid of your gas-powered mower and choose a reel mower or one powered by alternative fuels. You can tell that your mower has a two-cycle engine (less efficient than the newer four-cycle engines) if you add oil to your gas, and the engine does not have a dipstick.

According to the U. S. Environmental Protection Agency, the 54 million Americans mowing their lawns with gas-powered mowers each weekend contribute nearly 5 percent of the nation's air pollution.

Check with fast-food restaurants to find a supply of chip (french fry) fat to make into biofuel that can be used to run cars, tractors, and garden machinery. This waste product used to be given away free, but now that there is a proven demand for it, a small charge is not unusual.

At Nymans Garden (a National Trust Garden in Surrey, United Kingdom), all electric mowers and battery-powered equipment are recharged from solar panels. The tractor is run on locally produced, recycled vegetable oil.

One of the big advantages a lot of biofuels have over other fuel types is that they are relatively harmless to the environment if spilled.

Biofuels

Biofuels offer huge potential as alternative fuels to power garden machinery. Where biofuels are produced strictly from waste resources such as recycled vegetable oil, they represent a renewable energy source based on the carbon cycle. Agrofuels are far less sustainable, as these are made from crops grown specifically for fuel at the expense of food crops. This is a fast-moving area, with new ideas and research appearing all the time.

The manufacture of biofuels from algae is one very promising idea. Although we are still a long way off from being able to use algae to power our gardens, algae is definitely a fuel to keep an eye on for the future. The United States leads the field in algaculture research (the farming of algae). As early as 1978, when the Carter administration set up the Aquatic Species Program at the National Renewable Energy Laboratory (NREL) to investigate types of algae that could be grown for energy production, research suggested that farming algae in shallow ponds could supply enough biodiesel to completely replace fossil oil for all U.S. transportation and heating requirements. Since 1996, government funding has been reduced, so most of the research into growing algae for fuel is based in the private sector, where there are a number of exciting developments. Some companies are moving away from growing algae in ponds and toward vertical growing systems, which are claimed to help with problems of evaporation and wind-blown contamination.

In recent years the energy savings produced by alternative fuels has been called into question, with dispute about the amount of fossil-fuel energy required to grow and process agrofuels. Research is continuing into the myriad options for biofuel technology, but the basic principles are clear. If you stick to the simple premise of closing the circle, of converting waste material into fuel, you can't go too far wrong.

If you must use power tools

If you simply cannot give up your fuel-powered garden machinery, there are a couple of things you can do to reduce the damage to the environment. Make sure the engine is regularly tuned and serviced, and keep blades sharp for efficient cutting. Another way to reduce the damage is to use garden machinery in the late afternoon or early evening, as this will limit the exposure of emissions to sunlight, which converts pollutants to ozone.

13

Incorporating Advanced
Features and Ideas

In the past few years, designers and horticulturists in search of more sustainable ways to garden have begun to popularize concepts such as permaculture, green roofs, and rain gardens. If you put into practice the advice given thus far in the book, you will already have improved the green credentials of your garden considerably. But if you consider yourself a pioneer, you might want to try out some of the ideas described in this chapter. There is also a section here on fireproofing your garden, something you may be particularly interested in doing if you live in a vulnerable area.

Forest Gardening

Growing food sustainably is an important part of the greener garden. As we have seen, we can improve conventional methods for growing our own fruit and vegetables by capturing rainwater for irrigation, cutting down on pesticide use, and saving our own seeds. We can use crop rotation and green manures to return nutrients to the soil, and we can keep pests at bay by attracting natural predators. Traditional kitchen gardens are always going to be an intensive form of production and require lots of attention from us as gardeners, but there is another option.

A forest garden is a food production system inspired by the natural ecosystem of a young woodland or rain forest, with a wide range of crops grown in different vertical layers. It is a productive, low-maintenance way of growing crops, where nature does most of the work. Pioneered by Robert Hart in Shropshire in the 1960s, forest gardening combines the principle of companion planting with the idea of growing on multiple levels. A similar gardening practice has been popular in Kerela, Mali, for many years, where multi-level gardens of trees, vines, and livestock are intercropped with lower-level bushes, perennials, and root crops to provide the produce that supports a family.

In fact, this idea of using the established nature of perennials in preference over the intensive demands of annuals is popular around the world, and gardens based on similar principles can be found in Indonesia, Zambia, Zimbabwe, Tanzania, and Nepal. Critics have questioned whether multi-layered garden systems developed in the tropics are suitable for adaptation to a temperate climate, but research from Plants for a Future, the Agroforestry Research Trust, and the Central

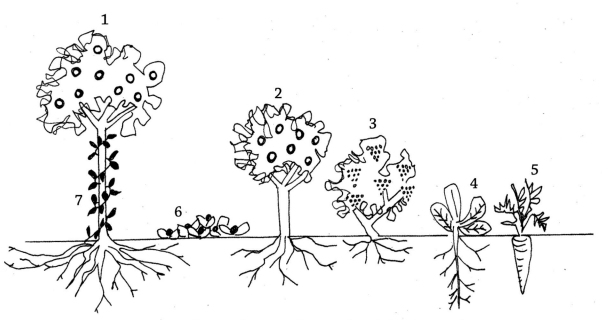

The seven layers of a forest garden system: **1.** canopy (large fruit and nut trees); **2.** low trees (dwarf fruit trees), **3.** shrubs (currants and berries); **4.** herbaceous plants (herbs, other plants); **5.** rhizosphere (roots); **6.** ground cover (such as strawberries); **7.** vertical layer (climbers and vines).

Rocky Mountain Permaculture Institute seem to be proving the critics wrong.

It is easy to see why the idea of forest gardening is so popular. Traditional vegetable plots (neat rows of annual crops that must be sown every year) demand a lot of time, attention, and resources, especially in relation to their yield. Growing a wider range of perennial plants can provide comparable cropping levels with much less effort—but you'll need a lot more room than your average allotment to be totally self-sufficient. The minimum you can get away with is probably 140 square metres (about 167 square yards) if you want to grow all the food you need for you and an average-sized family.

Hugh Fearnley-Whittingstall has done much to popularize the principles of forest gardening and permaculture in recent years, showing all the wonderful things we can do with the abundant seasonal resources around us. Plants for a Future also has spent many years researching plants with edible, medicinal, and other uses that might be part of an

GREEN TIP **To try out forest gardening, plant layers of edible plants from vines and tall trees down to shrubs, perennials, ground covers, and roots. Consider including edible plants conventionally grown as ornamentals, such as Oregon grape.**

ecologically sustainable environment based largely on perennial plants, and has created an excellent database from this ongoing research.

If you are keen to try out these ideas in your own garden, you'll need to plant layers of edible plants from vines and tall trees down to shrubs, perennials, ground covers, and roots. Include tall trees such as sweet chestnut and walnut, shorter trees such as apples, pears, and medlars (on a dwarfing rootstock), and then a shrub layer including currants, blackberries, and coppiced hazel. Underplant with perennials such as cardoons, rhubarb, wood sorrel, and wild garlic.

The key to a successful forest garden is not to limit yourself to traditional kitchen garden crops; many plants conventionally grown as ornamentals are also edible. For example, Oregon grape has edible fruits, the fresh shoots of bamboo are edible, and the shoots of Solomon's seal (*Polygonatum*) are rumoured to taste a bit like asparagus. In addition to an abundance of edible plants, you will need to include plants that

enhance the fertility of the soil (such as comfrey, clovers, and dogwood) and plants that encourage pollinating or beneficial insects.

Permaculture

Similar to forest gardening, permaculture is a design style that mimics natural ecosystems. First developed by Bill Mollison and David Holmgren in Australia in the 1970s, permaculture has as its basic principle the creation of closed-loop or self-sufficient systems. Key to permaculture is the idea of synergy, along with minimizing waste and limiting the demand for energy or labour as far as possible.

Creating natural plant communities and ecosystems is at the heart of permaculture. The rotation system in kitchen gardening is a simple example. Nitrogen-fixing legumes such as beans follow brassicas and leafy crops so that the nitrogen in the soil is restored before the next

(previous page) One of the simplest ways to make a forest garden is to convert an existing orchard—which gives you a head start on the canopy layer—by interplanting with additional trees and shrubs. Garden Collection/Andrew Lawson

(left) Embrace plants that you previously thought of as weeds; dandelion leaves are excellent in a mixed salad and their deep roots act as dynamic accumulators to make minerals in the soil available to more shallow-rooted plants. Garden Collection/Torie Chugg

(right) Hazel (hazelnut) produces nuts and building materials when grown after having been cut back. Garden Collection/ Derek St Romaine

(this page) With sufficient structural support you can create large-scale plantings as displayed by this fantastic roof garden in Rotherham, UK. Garden Collection/Jane Sebire

(next page top) Sedum is the most popular choice for planting a green roof because it looks good all year round. Garden Collection/ Liz Eddison

(next page bottom left) You don't have to stop at buildings. Try adding a green roof to your chicken coop, bird box, or beehive! Garden Collection/Nicola Stocken Tomkins

(next page bottom right) You can add a green roof to structure of any size. Here a green roof provides the finishing touch to a cob garden office. Clayworks/ Katy Bryce

PROJECT   Make a green roof

Whether you have acres of garden to play with or just a tiny courtyard, there is always room for a green roof. Think about adding a green roof to your garden shed or log store, chicken house, or even bird feeder. The structure doesn't have to have a flat top; a slope will happily accommodate a green roof, as long as the pitch is no more than 30 degrees. However you choose to incorporate a green roof into your garden design, the construction follows the same basic rules.

The first job is to make sure the structure you are planning to add a green roof to will be strong enough to support it—even when saturated with rainwater. In most cases, you will need to add extra vertical supports to your structure; these can be added to the inside or outside. You may also want to screw a sheet of plywood to the existing roof to strengthen it. The more weight you are adding to your roof, the more you will need to reinforce the structure at the start. If in doubt about the load-bearing potential, ask a professional for advice.

Next, add a waterproof membrane, using galvanized nails or staples to secure it along the edge of the roof. Measure each plane of your roof and construct a wooden frame to these exact dimensions to hold the substrate. The depth of your frame and substrate will depend on the plants you are planning to grow on your green roof. Sedum matting will grow on as little as 5 to 7 cm (2 to 3 in) of substrate, but you will need 10 to 25 cm (4 to 10 in) for a wildflower meadow.

If you are working on a small structure such as a birdhouse, you may want to build this frame directly onto the roof, but if you are working on a shed or larger structure, you will find it easier to construct your frame on the ground, then fix it to the roof. When creating a large green roof—for a shed or garden building—you will need to reinforce your frame with internal struts to create multiple pockets for the substrate to sit in. Aim for sections of no more than 50 × 50 cm (20 × 20 in) within the boundary of the frame; for example, a shed roof 2 × 1 m (roughly 1 × 2.5 yd) would ideally hold a grid of six sections.

Once you are happy with your frame, get some help lifting it into place and secure it to the roof using more galvanized nails. If you are working with a sloping roof, you might find it easiest to nail the frame to the strong vertical posts you used to reinforce the structure of the building. Fill the frame with your chosen substrate—crushed brick, limestone, or perlite are popular choices. Then plant your plugs or seeds—or lay your sedum mats. Water until saturated.

year-round, changing colour through green, pink, and purple without going through the scruffy phase that grasses and herbaceous plants can suffer from—and without needing cutting back.

There are several types of green roofs:

SEDUM MATS. Sedum mats are pregrown and delivered to the site like a rolled-up carpet. The mats are laid on 5 to 7 cm (2 to 3 in) of growing medium (the standard method) or directly onto a moisture-retention blanket (the ultralightweight method).

SUBSTRATE-BASED ROOFS. 7 cm (3 in) of crushed aggregate, limestone, perlite, or recycled brick is placed on the green roof system and plug planted with sedums or with sedum mats. Some green roofs are made of turf, but this is not generally the case in the United Kingdom.

GREEN OR BROWN ROOFS FOR BIODIVERSITY. These are like substrate-based roofs but can use recycled aggregate from on-site and are generally left to colonize naturally or seeded with an annual wildflower mix.

Green Walls

We all know how dramatic the addition of a climber can be, adding height and lush greenery to a garden. Green walls represent the next logical step, taking advantage of the commonly overlooked vertical plane. A green wall is essentially a green roof turned on its side. It combines all the benefits of green roofs with all the beauty of a well-managed climber—and the best systems look after and irrigate themselves.

A green wall offers these advantages:

* reduces heating and air conditioning requirements (and costs)

* reduces the heat island effect

* absorbs rainwater to help reduce flooding

* purifies the air

* reduces noise

* offers habitat for biodiversity

(left) The plants that can be used to make your living wall vary depending on the location and site conditions, but you can plant leafy green vegetables and herbs for a vertical kitchen garden.

(right) Although most green facades make use of evergreen climbers, even the bare matrix formed by the stems of deciduous climbers (such as wisteria or climbing hydrangea) can trap air and insulate a building.

GREEN TIP **Invest in a professional system and try planting ajuga, lirope, ivy, sedum, heuchera, or euphorbia in a living wall. These can be used to make complex patterns or can be arranged simply in swathes or swirls.**

There are two types of green walls:

GREEN FACADES. Green facades give climbers the necessary support to create a green screen on the side of a building while still keeping their roots in the ground. Stainless or galvanized steel fittings are most commonly used to hold a matrix of tensioned wire away from the building so that the fabric of the building remains undamaged by the plants and so that trapped air insulates the building. Shipping fixtures are often used to create green facades, but there are custom-made systems available.

LIVING WALLS. Living walls are integral systems that usually grow plants in a modular hydroponic-fed system. They are often installed to clad all or part of a building, and include a trapped air space, just like a green facade. Many living wall systems have been designed to use grey water or storm water to directly irrigate their plantings.

It is difficult to create a green wall that will be healthy and self-sustaining for any length of time without the help of a professional system. There are a number of low-tech systems available (without irrigation), but I have never seen these succeed for more than a few months. Where green walls are concerned, you really do get what you pay for. If you are serious about including a green wall in your garden, invest in a professional system that includes irrigation and nutrition. If you get the system right from the start, you will be rewarded with a sumptuous, low-maintenance green wall that is the envy of your neighbours. Try and create a green wall on the cheap, and you'll have a very sad-looking wall of crusty, dying foliage within a matter of months.

PROJECT Create a rain garden

The first thing to do is to dig an infiltration pit to see how quickly water drains away naturally in your garden. Dig a hole 30 × 30 cm (1 × ×1 ft) and fill it with a bucket of water to see how quickly it sinks into the soil. Sandy soils will drain away quickly, but if you have a lot of clay in your soil and it drains very slowly, you may want to add organic matter or aggregate to your planting depression.

Then dig a flat-bottomed saucer shape (which will hold more water than a bowl shape) 15 to 20 cm (6 to 8 in) deep. When the rain garden is full of water, the plants will be sitting in saturated soil for hours or even days, so choose pond edge plants like sedges,

reeds and that can withstand extremes of both flooding and drought. Remember — plants which are used to moist soil will do far better than plants which have adapted for drought so look towards penstemon, salix, persicaria, ferns, and ornamental grasses for the basis of your planting scheme. The list of potential rain garden plants is vast so don't be afraid to experiment (see bimodal planting in chapter 9 for more ideas). Once you have planted your rain garden, you might like to mulch it with aggregate or larger stones, as these will slow down any storm water even further and give a neat finish to your planted depression.

Rain Gardens

It is important to use water sustainably in our changing climate, and we have already seen some good ways to use rainwater more effectively in our gardens: incorporating permeable surfaces, harvesting water, grouping plants according to their watering requirements, choosing storm-tolerant plants, and using bioswales to cope with floodwater. Rain gardens are an extension of these principles—in essence, gardens that are specifically designed to manage storm water runoff.

At first glance, a rain garden may look like just another pretty garden, but look again. Rain gardens are usually sited close to a source of runoff; these planted depressions can slow the water, reducing the risk of erosion and giving the storm water more time to infiltrate into the soil. Most of the time rain gardens are dry, but when there is a deluge they can slow and hold large amounts of water. They can be described as dry, planted ponds, but I prefer to think of them as sponges, collecting water when there is a storm and drying out over the course of the next few days.

Rain gardens also tackle the problem of polluted storm water, which is often high in nitrogen and phosphorous. Unlike rainwater, storm water collects all sorts of pollutants from our gardens, driveways, and

Phytoremediation—that is, the use of plants for decontamination—is not a new idea. It has been used for many years to clean up industrial sites that have been abandoned as a result of environmental contamination. After the Chernobyl accident, for example, sunflowers were planted to extract uranium from the soil.

streets—anything from spilt fuel to detergents, grease, heavy metals, and fertilizer. As the water passes through the rain garden, the plants filter and clean it. Reeds and irises are among the plants popularly used in rain gardens to help remove many of these toxins along with any sediment the storm water has collected. The best results are achieved when several rain gardens are designed in sequence, each one slowing and cleaning the water a little more.

Rain gardens can be as simple as a deep trough at the base of a drainpipe or as complex as a series of bioswales; either way, the idea is to create planted depressions where water can be held for a few hours while it drains away into the soil. As a general rule, rain gardens should not hold water for more than a few days—ideally they should dry out within 24 to 48 hours. If you already have areas of your garden that collect water after heavy rainfall, take a tip from nature and think about creating your rain garden there—it will save you the job of redirecting your runoff.

Natural Swimming Ponds

A natural swimming pool, or swimming pond, is the green alternative to a traditional swimming pool. Natural swimming pools rely on aquatic and marginal plants—instead of chlorine, salt, or ozone—to keep the water clean and crystal clear. If the pond is managed properly, there is no need for an electric UV filter.

Natural swimming pools usually contain two basic areas: the swimming zone and the regeneration zone. The regeneration zone is a marginal area containing oxygenating aquatic plants such as *Ceratophyllum* and *Elodea* and marginal plants such as sedge, iris, pitcher plant, rushes, and reeds planted in aggregate or shingle. The regeneration zone is usually at least as big as the swimming zone. The swimming zone is very similar to a conventional swimming pool. It can include a deep swimming area with stone or tiled walls.

Natural swimming pools need to be much larger overall than chemically treated pools since about half of the pool is devoted to plants. Walls separating the planting area of the pool from the swimming area usually end at least 10 cm (4 in) below the surface of the water to ensure a seamless look. Usually a solar-powered pump is used to circulate water between the swimming and regeneration zones.

(top left) A natural swimming pool can be designed to look like a natural pool or lake so that it blends seamlessly with the countryside around it like this one at Wolfram Kircher's garden in Germany. Jane Sebire

(top right) Some natural swimming pools are uncompromisingly minimalist in their design, such as this rectangular lap pool designed by Clear Water Revival. Clear Water Revival

(bottom left) Marginal plants can be decorative, too, such as these lovely irises planted in the regeneration zone. Clear Water Revival

(bottom right) Reeds and rushes help to filter and clean the water. The regeneration zone containing these plants is usually at least as large (in volume) as the swimming pool itself.

Natural swimming pools cost about the same to build as conventional swimming pools, but they have much lower maintenance costs. Existing ponds and swimming pools can even be converted into natural swimming pools (but you'll need an expert to help).

Hydroponics and Aquaponics

Hydroponics is a method of growing plants without soil. Instead, plants get their nutrition from minerals dissolved in water. Hydroponics is becoming increasingly important for food production because compared to traditional row cropping it produces higher crop yields, takes up less space, recycles its nutrients effectively, and suffers less from problems with pests, weeds, or disease.

Aquaponics takes this idea one step further. In aquaponics, fish and plants grow together in one integrated, soilless system. The fish waste provides a food source for the plants, and the plants provide a natural filter for the water the fish live in. Aquaponics produces safe, fresh organic fish and vegetables.

In an aquaponics scheme, bacteria in the grow beds break down the waste ammonia from the fish tank into nitrites and nitrates. The nitrates feed the plants while the plant roots and planting medium filter the water that is on its way back to the fish tank. The water needs to be oxygenated by a pump as oxygen is essential for both the fish and the plants to grow happily.

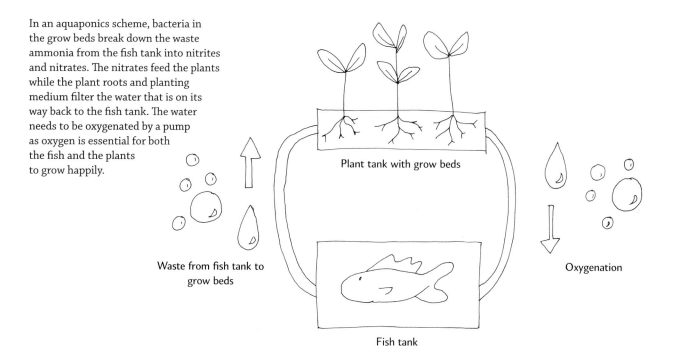

Plant tank with grow beds

Waste from fish tank to grow beds

Oxygenation

Fish tank

If you fancy building your own aquaponics system, it's often best to start with a simple 10- or 20-gallon aquarium (available from your local pet shop). Line the bottom of your tank with washed gravel (allow just over 1 kg—or roughly 2 lb—gravel for every 5 gallons of water). You'll also need an air pump (to oxygenate the water) and a small water pump to move water from the fish tank to the growing bed. Your growing bed, which will sit on top of the tank, can be anything from an old planter to a recycled container; just make sure it's a little bit bigger than the footprint of the tank so it will sit firmly on top.

Drill some small holes in the bottom of the growing bed so that water can drain back into the tank, plus one larger hole for the water pump tube. With the water pump sitting in the tank, feed the tubing up through the large hole and into the growing bed. Loop this tubing around the inside of the growing bed and trim off any excess. Seal the end with electrical tape and fill this container with growing medium (gravel, expanded clay pebbles, or perlite) until it is level with the top of the tubing. Pierce a series of small holes in the top surface of the tubing that sits in the growing bed (so this will be a bit like perforated pipe irrigation). Cover the tubing with another couple of inches of your chosen growing medium.

Now fill your tank with water. Check the pump is circulating water continuously from the tank up into the growing bed and then trickling back down through the growing medium into the tank. You may have to adjust the pump to get the right rate of flow. Turn on the air pump and let it run for twenty-four hours before you add your fish to ensure there is no chlorine in the water.

You should initially stock your tank with ½ inch of fish per gallon (although you can double this after the first month). Most home aquaponics systems will not be large enough to accommodate fish that can be grown for food, so many novices start with goldfish. If your system is large enough, you might choose to stock popular food fish such as tilapia, perch, cod, or trout. You will need to feed your fish daily and refill the tank to the top every few days to replace water lost by evaporation.

After a month, you will be able to add plants to your aquaponics system. Leafy vegetables such as spinach, herbs, and lettuces are good crops to start with, although established systems can support peas and beans—and even tomatoes. For best results sow directly into your growing bed. If you are planning to transplant seedlings, make sure you wash all of the soil from the roots before adding them to your growing bed.

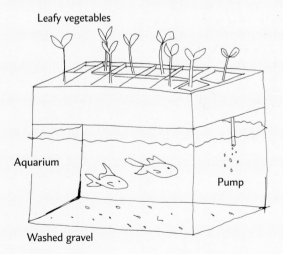

Place a growing bed on top of a 10- or 20-gallon aquarium and stock it with fish to get your home aquaponics system going.

GREEN TIP **Think about buying a kit if you want to set up an aquaponics system. In the United States, suppliers include Nelson and Pade (www.aquaponics. com), AquaponicsUSA (www. aquaponicsUSA.com), and Earth Solutions (www.earthsolutions. com); U.K. stockists include Aquaponics UK (aquaponics.org. uk).**

Although the basic principle is pretty simple, creating your own aquaponics system can be a little more complex, so many gardeners choose to buy a kit rather than construct their own system from scratch. The two most common systems are media-filled beds (popular with backyard enthusiasts) and the raft system (the commercial standard).

The media-filled bed system uses a tank or container filled with perlite, gravel, or other aggregate to grow plant crops. A second tank is full of fish (don't forget the aeration pump). Water from the fish tanks is periodically used to flood the plant bed and then allowed to drain back into the fish tank. All waste (including solids) is broken down in the plant bed and feeds the plants. This simple system may need cleaning periodically as solid waste buildup can reduce the plants' ability to take up nutrients over time.

The raft system is a little more complicated to set up but a lot more productive and efficient once it is up and running. Plants are grown on polystyrene boards that float on top of the water, with their roots sitting directly in the water. Fish are usually contained in a second tank. Water flows continuously between the tanks (passing through a filter as it does). Raft systems are often more expensive to install than a simple media-bed system, but they are much more efficient. The raft prevents weeds and evaporation, allows higher stocking densities of fish, and as long as the filter is working effectively, does not need cleaning.

Fireproofing

A well-designed garden can help to keep you safe from the risk of wildfires. In hot weather, when gardens and vegetation are dry, flames and embers can ignite plants and garden structures within seconds. Choosing fireproof materials when constructing your garden, including access to water, and using plants that resist burning are some of the simplest ways to fireproof your garden and protect your home.

The first thing to consider when designing a fireproof garden is to create a firebreak around the property. Flammable materials such as decking should be replaced with lawn, low ground cover, stone, gravel, or pebbles to a distance of at least 1.5 m (1.64 yd). Whichever material you choose, try to create a permeable surface that will allow water to infiltrate into the ground.

Next, think about any garden structures such as pergolas, fences, benches, or garden buildings. Avoid fixing these directly to the house, choose a noncombustible material where possible, and cover them with climbing or rambling plants that have low flammability. The fleshy, evergreen star jasmine (*Trachelospermum jasminoides*) is a good choice that recovers well even if it does get burned. Other good choices include grape, climbing roses, and (perhaps surprisingly) wisteria. It is always tempting to locate a seat or bench in a sunny spot up against the house, but in a fireproof garden it is best to bring it forward, out of the firebreak zone, or at least make sure it is not wooden.

An independent water supply is another useful defence against fire, so make sure you include plenty of provision for water barrels, tanks, and ponds. Swimming pools are another useful source of water in an emergency. These water features should be placed on the side of the property that is most at risk. (If in doubt, use the prevailing wind direction as your guide.)

Compost heaps and woodpiles should be located as far away from buildings as possible, and away from trees or flammable structures. In fire-prone areas, you might want to consider keeping these flammable features inside a metal shed for extra protection.

Once all the structural elements are in place, it's time to think about the planting in a bit more detail. No plant is completely fire resistant, but some plants are more flammable than others. Obvious plants to avoid include trees with loose or peeling bark, plants with a high oil or resin content (these are often aromatic), and plants that accumulate large amounts of dead branches, needles, or leaves (so avoid pines, beech, hornbeam, and the like). You can usually spot plants that are resistant to fire by looking out for broad fleshy leaves, smooth bark, and compact dense foliage. Fire-retardant plants include daphne, flowering quince, hebe, nandina, pittosporum, silk-tassel, and weigela.

As a general rule, plants close to the house need to be lower-growing and more widely spaced than conventional rules dictate. As you mover farther and farther away from the property, you will be able to indulge in large plants at close spacing. Where plants are close to the house, they should be low ground covers such as ajuga and viola. As you move farther away from the house and plants get taller and closer together, avoid the temptation to plant in large unbroken blocks. Instead, plant

GREEN TIP **Fireproof your garden by creating a firebreak around your property, choosing fireproof materials, including access to water, and using plants that resist burning.**

(top left) Star jasmine (*Trachelospermum jasminoides*) is a sterling choice for a fireproof planting scheme. It has low flammability and recovers well even if it does get burned.

(top right) No plant is completely fire resistant, but some plants are less flammable than others. The compact succulent leaves of drought-tolerant senecio make it a good choice for a fire-resistant planting scheme.

(bottom left) The broad fleshy leaves and compact dense foliage of sedum make it a fire-retardant plant.

(bottom right) Hebe is remarkably hard to burn and is an excellent choice for a fireproof planting.

in small, irregular clusters or islands broken up by gravel or stone pathways that will act as additional firebreaks. You can avoid creating a "fire ladder effect" where the staggered heights of plants provide continuous fuel from the ground right up into the tree canopy by remembering to include a gap between the top of a shrub and the lowest branches of a nearby tree so that it is harder for fire to jump between plants.

Trees are important in any garden and should not be excluded from the fireproof landscape scheme. Instead a few simple precautions should be taken. Trees should never be planted too close to the house where they might overhang the roof or guttering (this avoids a buildup of dry fallen leaves, which are highly flammable). Plant them farther away from the house, with a wider than usual spacing so that the crowns do not touch. Many trees with smooth bark, such as apple trees, *Cercis siliquastrum*, and evergreen oaks, are often a good choice (although there are obvious exceptions such as eucalyptus). Prune away any low-hanging branches, giving each tree a clear stem up to at least 1.5 m (5 ft).

A Compost-Based Energy Supply

This final advanced idea relates to the concept of using waste products in a closed-loop system. The French innovator Jean Pain (1930–1981) developed a compost-based closed-loop system that supplied him with 100 percent of his energy needs. The Jean Pain method is based on some very simple principles and is easy to replicate.

A 50-tonne steel tank (capacity 4 cubic metres) is filled with compost that has been steeped in water for two months. This tank is hermetically sealed and connected by tubing to twenty-four inner truck tyres. A 200-m (218-yd) plastic tube is wrapped around the tank before more compost is mounded up around the steel tank.

As the compost ferments, the methane produced collects in the inner tubes. It takes about ninety days to produce 500 cubic metres of gas (enough to keep two ovens and three burner stoves going for a year). Jean Pain used a methane-fueled combustion engine to turn a generator (100 watts per hour) that charged an accumulative battery. This battery stored the current, providing all the light needed for the household.

Hot water is generated through the plastic tubing buried inside the compost mound. Heat from the composting process can produce up to

4 litres (1 gallon) per minute of hot water at 60 degrees C (140 degrees F), which supplies all the central heating plus washing requirements.

After about eighteen months, the compost will be ready—at which point you can dismantle the structure, use the lovely compost, and start the process all over again.

Jean Pain was a French innovator who developed a closed-loop system that supplied him with 100 percent of his energy requirements.

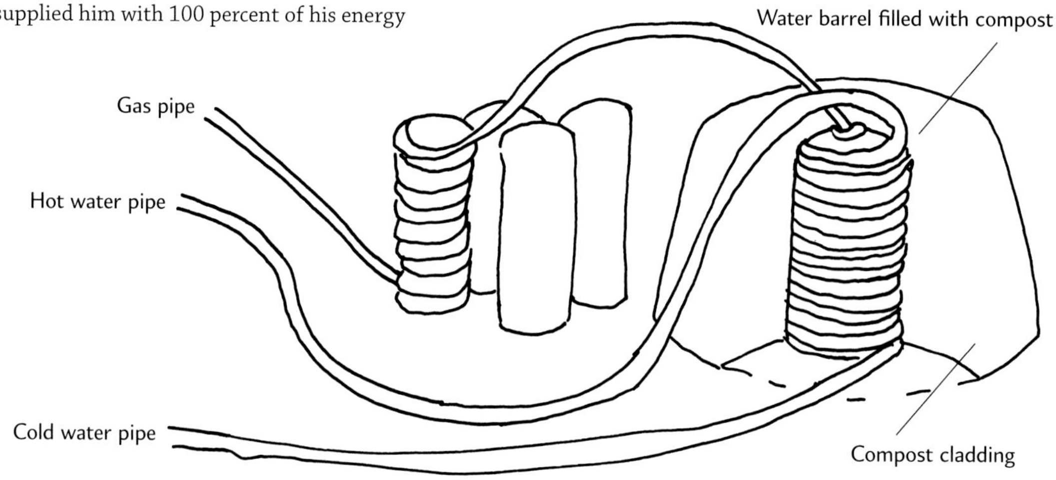

Gas pipe

Hot water pipe

Cold water pipe

Water barrel filled with compost

Compost cladding

GLOSSARY

ADOBE A building material that is made from clay, sand, and straw and is usually formed into bricks that are then dried in the sun.

AGGREGATE A material or structure formed from a mass of fragments or particles that are loosely compacted together, such as gravel or stone chippings.

AGROFUEL Fuel that is made from the oil in plant crops.

ANAEROBIC COMPOSTING The process of composting without oxygen; using a compost bin that is not aerated.

ANOXIA The absence of oxygen.

AQUAPONICS The process of growing plants and aquatic animals together in a mutually beneficial environment.

ARTHROPOD An invertebrate with a segmented body, external skeleton, and jointed limbs.

BIMODAL PLANTS Plants which can tolerate more than one type of weather extreme.

BIODIVERSITY A variety of plant and animal life in either a particular place or the world.

BIOSWALE A wide, gradually sloping landscape element that is filled with compost, vegetation, and/or rocks and is built to remove silt and other pollutants from surface runoff water.

BOKASHI A process of composting in which kitchen scraps are fermented using microorganisms such as yeast and other kinds of bacteria.

CEMENT A powder that is made by heating lime and clay.

CLOSED LOOP SYSTEM Reusing materials that are found either on or very near to the site, thus engaging in self-sufficient construction.

COB A building material that is based on a mixture of clay, sand, and straw.

COIR Coconut fibre.

COMPOST TEA A liquid compost produced by soaking compost in water. It can be used as a soil drench or as a foliar feed.

CONCRETE A mixture of cement, water, and other aggregates, such as sand and/or gravel.

COPPICE, COPPICING A traditional method for managing forests by repeatedly cutting woodland trees down to ground level and allowing them to reshoot; coppiced trees growing together in a small wood or forest.

DIPSTICK A graduated rod for measuring the depth of a liquid.

EARTH BAG CONSTRUCTION A process in which fabric bags are filled with soil, rice hulls, other aggregates, or any other plentiful material, and used for construction.

ECOSYSTEM A biological community of interacting organisms and their physical environment.

EMBODIED ENERGY The total amount of energy required to create, transport, and dispose of an item. Sometimes also referred to as "cradle to grave."

ENERGY RETURNED ON ENERGY INVESTED A calculation of the total energy consumed and released over a product's lifetime.

ERICACEOUS Plants that are of the heather family and grow well in acidic, lime-free soils.

ESPALIER A method of training plants to grow against a flat structure, or the actual structure that the plants are trained against, such as a wall, trellis, or other framework.

FASCINE OR FAGGOT A bundle of sticks used to strengthen banks or fill ditches.

FIREPROOFING Ensuring an object is able to withstand fire or great heat.

FOREST GARDENING The cultivation of a food production system based on natural woodland eco-systems.

FOSSIL FUEL A natural fuel that is created from decomposed remains of living organisms.

GABION A wickerwork or metal cage that is filled with earth, stones, rubble, or any other material to create walls, structures, and other building fortifications.

GLAUCOUS Describes the colour of dull greyish-green or blue foliage.

GRASSCRETE A cellular support system for a lawn or paving which is usually constructed from concrete or plastic.

GREYWATER Nonseptic domestic wastewater generated through activities such as laundry, washing up, or bathing that can be reused on-site for landscape irrigation.

HA-HA A ditch with a wall on its inner side below ground level, forming a boundary to a park or garden without interrupting the view.

HEMPCRETE A cementlike mixture of hemp and lime that can be used for construction.

HERBACEOUS With a stem that has little or no woody tissue, usually living for a single growing season.

HORTICULTURAL VINEGAR An acetic acid that is four times stronger than household vinegar and can be used as an organic, nonselective weed-killer.

HYDROPONICS The process of growing plants in sand, gravel, or liquid, with added nutrients but without soil.

INVERTED GARDENING Upside-down gardening, where the pot and growing medium are suspended upside down and the plant grows downward.

LEAF MOULD A compost produced from the fungal decomposition of deciduous leaves.

LIVE CRIB WALL A three-dimensional structure, created from untreated timbers, fill, and live cuttings, which acts as a retaining wall.

MICROCLIMATE The climate of a very small or restricted area, especially when this differs from the climate of the surrounding area.

METHANE A colourless, odourless, flammable gas which is the main component of natural gas.

MORTISE AND TENON JOINTS A device that is used to join pieces of timber without using nails or glue. The tenon (tongue) fits into the mortise (hole) at a 90 degree angle to create a strong joint that can be used for many garden structures.

NEMATODES Microscopic worms that are often found in soil.

PATHOGEN A microorganism, bacterium, or virus that can cause disease.

PEAT Partly decomposed vegetable matter which forms deposits on acidic, boggy ground, which is then dried and used in gardening and as a fuel.

PERCOLATE To filter or pass through a porous substance.

PERLITE Naturally occurring volcanic glass which has an ability to hold huge amounts of air and water.

PERMACULTURE The development of agricultural ecosystems that are intended to be sustainable and self-sufficient.

PERMEABLE A state in which liquids and gases may pass through a substance.

PHYTOREMEDIATION The process by which plant-based systems remove, degrade, or stabilize organic and inorganic contaminants in environments.

PLANT COMMUNITIES Groups of plants that are assembled to interact with each other as well as with the elements of their environment while remaining distinct from adjacent groups.

PLANT GUILD A plant combination that is stronger together than as its individual components.

POLE SLING A device that uses two long poles and a sling to distribute the weight of an object and make it easy to carry.

POLLARD A method of pruning that can be used to control the height of trees. A pollarded tree is cut back at intervals to a desired place on the main stem and then allowed to regrow.

RAIN CHAIN A device that collects rainwater and directs it down a chain towards the ground, functioning as an alternative to a traditional gutter downspout.

RAIN GARDEN A planted depression that collects rainwater runoff and allows it to absorb gradually into the soil.

RAMMED EARTH A building process that uses damp, compressed earth that is shaped by wooden shuttering and is then allowed to dry, creating walls and structures.

RECLAIMED Material recovered for reuse; recycled.

ROTOVATE OR ROTOTILL To till or break up soil using a Rotavator or Rototiller machine.

SHELTERBELT A line of trees and shrubs that are planted to slow damaging winds and protect an area.

SPIGOT A tap or a valve.

STEM WALL A supporting structure that connects the foundation of a building with its vertical walls.

STEPPE A large area of flat. unforested grassland.

STOLON A horizontal stem that produces the roots and shoots of a new plant.

STOMATA Minute pores found on the leaves and/or stems of plants.

SUBSTRATE An underlying substance or layer.

SUCKER A shoot growing from the base of a plant.

SUPER ADOBE A type of construction in which long, thin fabric bags are filled with adobe and used as a building material.

SWALE A low, moist tract of land with gently sloping sides that has a natural or manmade open drainage system to manage water runoff.

SYSTEMS THINKING *see* WHOLE SYSTEM THINKING

THATCH Plant materials that are used for roofing.

URBANITE Broken pieces of concrete that are reused without being fully recycled into a new material.

WASTE HIERARCHY A system in which the different ways of disposing of waste are ranked in order to foster sustainability and environmental benefits.

WATER TABLE The underground depth at which point the ground becomes completely saturated with water.

WHOLE SYSTEM THINKING The process of understanding how things influence one another within a whole.

WHORL Spiral or circular growth in plants.

WITHIES Tough but flexible branches of an osier or other willow that are used for tying, binding or basketry.

XERISCAPE A garden or landscape that requires little or no supplementary watering.

REFERENCES AND RESOURCES

1: IMPROVING YOUR GARDEN'S ECOLOGICAL CREDENTIALS

BRE Green Guide to Specification. www.bre.co.uk/greenguide/podpage.jsp?id=2126. Online guide from the U.K. firm BRE Global Ltd. to the relative environmental impacts (based on life cycle analysis) of building and landscape materials.

Freecycle Network. www.freecycle.org. Global nonprofit, grassroots organization connecting people who are giving and getting free stuff to keep it out of landfills.

Recycle-more. www.recycle-more.co.uk. One-stop recycling information centre, offering advice on all aspects of recycling in the United Kingdom.

Sustainable Sites Initiative. www.sustainablesites.org. U.S. effort to create voluntary national guidelines and performance benchmarks for sustainable land design, construction, and maintenance practices.

Sustainable and Urban Gardening. www.sustainable-gardening.com. Website with the purpose of teaching gardening in a sustainable, environmentally responsible way, authored mainly by Susan Harris of Maryland, United States.

World Commission on Environment and Development.1987. *Our Common Future* (also referred to as the Brundtland Commission report). Oxford: Oxford University Press.

Yestermorrow Design/Build School. yestermorrow.org. School in Vermont offering courses in sustainable landscape design.

Note: Internet links change frequently. If a link no longer works, try using the organisation's or publication's name in your web browser.

2: HANDLING WATER AND WASTE

Water

Dewees, Amanda. 2006. Improving landscape irrigation efficiency. Presentation to the American Water Works Association Water Sources Conference 2006. www.awwa.org/waterwiser/references/pdfs/RES_LSCAPE_Dewees_A_Improving_Landscape_Irrigation_Efficiency.pdf.

Irrigation Association. Smart irrigation month: Water wisely. Simple strategies to save water and money and see better results. www.irrigation.org/Resources/Smart_Irrigation_Month/Consumer_Water_Wisely.aspx.

Rainharvesting Systems. www.rainharvesting.co.uk. U.K. company that designs and supplies systems to collect rain for home and garden use.

Sustainable Landscape Council. www.sustainablelandscapecouncil.com/images/droughtpresentation.pdf. Presentation on how to help your lawn through a drought.

Waste

Bruce, Maye. 1946. *Common-Sense Compost Making by the Quick Return Method*. London: Faber & Faber. Revised edition, 2009, Bingfield, Newcastle Upon Tyne: QR Composting Solutions.

Cleeve Nursery. www.cleevenursery.co.uk/page.php?id=10. U.K. Retail outlet supplying gardeners with compost tea.

Davenport, Andrew. 2008. *Quick Return Compost Making: The Essence of the Sustainable Organic Garden*. Bingfield, Newcastle Upon Tyne: QR Composting Solutions.

Durham, Sharon. 2006. Recommendations for a safer compost tea. USDA Agricultural Research Service. www.ars.usda.gov/is/pr/2006/060921.htm.

Edgerton, S. A., M.A.K. Khalil, and R. A. Rasmussen. 1984. Estimates of air pollution from backyard burning. *Journal of the Air Pollution Control Association* 34: 661–64.

Half of U.S. food goes to waste. 25 November 2004. Foodproductiondaily.com. www.foodproductiondaily.com/Supply-Chain/Half-of-US-food-goes-to-waste.

Ingham, Elaine. 2010. *The Compost Tea Brewing Manual*, 5th ed. Corvallis, OR: Soil Foodweb Inc.

Lemieux, P. M., C. C. Lutes, and D. A. Santoianni. 2004. Emissions of organic air toxics from open burning. *Progress in Energy and Combustion Science* 30: 1–34.

We Don't Waste Food! A Householder Survey. March 2007. Waste and Resources Action Programme. www.wrap.org.uk/downloads/We_don_t_ waste_food_-_A_household_survey_mar_07.e8afefec.6397.pdf.

3: PICKING MATERIALS FOR PATHS AND PAVING

Chalker-Scott, Linda. The myth of rubberized landscapes. http://www. puyallup.wsu.edu/~linda%20chalker-scott/horticultural%20myths_files/ Myths/Rubber%20mulch.pdf.

Ethical Trading Initiative. www.ethicaltrade.org. Alliance of companies, trade unions, and voluntary organisations dedicated to improving the working lives of people who make consumer goods across the globe. The ETI Base Code establishes minimum standards for working conditions.

IEA Clean Coal Centre. 2005. Cement and concrete—benefits and barriers in coal fly ash utilisation. www.greenspec.co.uk/documents/ materials/cementsub/flyash.pdf.

India Committee of the Netherlands. 2006. *From Quarry to Graveyard: Corporate Social Responsibility in the Natural Stone Sector*. www.indianet. nl/fromquarrytograveyard.html.

International Energy Agency (IEA) and World Business Council for Sustainable Development. 2009. *Cement Technology Roadmap 2009*. Paris: IEA. www.wbcsd.org/DocRoot/mka1EKor6mqLVb9w903o/WBCSD-IEA_ CementRoadmap.pdf.

Mine Labour Protection Campaign. mlpc.in. Nongovernmental organisation working to oganize mine labourers in the state of Rajasthan in India to protect their rights and the environment.

4: COVERING GROUND WITH DECKS AND LAWNS

Decks

Environmental Investigation Agency. 2008. *Borderlines: Vietnam's Booming Furniture Industry and Timber Smuggling in the Mekong Region*. www.eia-global.org/PDF/reports--borderlines--forests--Feb08.pdf.

Forest Stewardship Council. www.fsc.org. Certifies sustainably grown and harvested timber.

FSC-Watch. www.fsc-watch.org. Independent observer of the Forest Stewardship Council with an excellent website that highlights potential problems with suppliers.

Green Wood Centre. www.greenwoodcentre.org.uk. Offers courses in woodland management and making outdoor furniture from local FSC timber.

Intergovernmental Panel on Climate Change (IPCC) Working Group I. 2007. *Climate Change 2007: The Physical Science Basis: Summary for Policy Makers*. Paris: IPCC Secretariat.

Programme for the Endorsement of Forest Certification (PEFC). www.pefc.org. Certifies sustainably grown and harvested timber.

Recycle Wood. www.recyclewood.org.uk. Offers a database of recycled wood products and a wood recycling service.

Seneca Creek Associates and Wood Resources International. 2004. *"Illegal" Logging and Global Wood Markets: The Competitive Impacts on the U.S. Wood Products Industry*. www.illegal-logging.info/uploads/afandpa.pdf.

Sherrill, Sam. *Harvesting Urban Timber: A Guide to Making Better Use of Urban Trees*. Fresno, CA: Linden Publishing, 2003.

Timber Trade Federation. www.ttf.co.uk. Trade association for the timber industry and timber companies, arguing the case for timber products as the only truly renewable building resource. Offers advice and information sheets on global timber policies and political developments.

U.S. Green Building Council. www.usgbc.org. Offers LEED (Leadership in Energy and Environmental Design) certification, verifying that buildings meet the highest green building and performance standards.

Wood for Good. www.woodforgood.com. Provides facts about wood sustainability and the environment, as well as wood experts and suppliers.

World Wildlife Fund. *Illegal Wood for the European Market*. 2008. www.wwf.dk/dk/Service/Bibliotek/Skov/Rapporter+mv./Illegal+Wood+for+the+European+Market.

Lawns
Castle, Rosemary. 2001. *Liberating Lawns*. Gloucestershire: Alternative Plants.

Daniels, Stevie. 1997. *The Wild Lawn Handbook: Alternatives to the Traditional Front Lawn*. New York: Macmillan.

Haeg, Fritz. 2008. *Edible Estates: Attack on the Front Lawn*. Los Angeles: Metropolis Books.

Healthy Lawns, Healthy Families. www.healthylawns.org. Website put up by the Oregon Department of Environmental Quality to educate about natural lawn care.

Jenkins, Virginia Scott. 1994. *The Lawn: A History of An American Obsession*. Washington, DC: Smithsonian Books.

Pollan, Michael. May 28, 1989. Why mow? The case against lawns. *New York Times Magazine*. www.michaelpollan.com/article.php?id=33.

Rocky Mountain Sod Farms. www.rockymountainsod.com. Supplier of wildflower turf in the United States.

Smaller American Lawns Today (SALT). conncoll.edu/ccrew/greennet/arbo/salt/salt.html. Movement aimed at reducing the lawn mania in America.

5: CHOOSING MATERIALS FOR BOUNDARIES AND STRUCTURES

Hedges
National Hedgelaying Society. www.hedgelaying.org.uk. Organisation committed to conserving hedgerows through traditional skills, offering training in the United Kingdom.

Willow

Cornish Willow. www.cornishwillow.co.uk/courses.htm. Offers courses in willow skills.

English Basketry Willows. www.englishbasketrywillows.com. Aims to provide a complete resource on willow basketry and living willow structures.

Essex Willow. www.essexwillow.co.uk/workshops.htm. Growers and suppliers of willow for bio-engineering. Offers willow workshops.

Musgrove Willows. www.willowcourses.com. Runs a range of courses in willow making throughout the year.

Out to Learn Willow. www.outtolearnwillow.co.uk. Provides both living willow and dried willow workshops for adults, children and young people.

Sylvan Skills. www.sylvanskills.co.uk. Offers willow workshops, courses, and demonstrations in Hexham, Northumberland.

Willow Bank. www.thewillowbank.com. Willow specialists in do-it-yourself kits and courses.

Fences

Weald and Downland Open Air Museum. www.wealddown.co.uk/Courses/courses-countryside-skills.htm. Offers a course in coppice management.

Cob and rammed earth

California Institute of Earth Art and Architecture. calearth/org. Nonprofit organisation in California teaching earthbag construction.

Clayworks. www.clay-works.com. Manufacturer of clay blocks and clay plasters in Cornwall.

Earth Architecture. eartharchitecture.org. Source of information about books and courses on earth architecture.

Natural Homes. naturalhomes.org. Clearinghouse for information about straw bale, cob, adobe, earthbag, and other natural means of home construction.

Rael, Ronald. 2010. *Earth Architecture*. Princeton, NJ: Princeton Architectural Press.

Seven Generations Natural Builders. www.sgnb.com. Offers workshops in natural building skills: cob, straw bale, natural plasters, woodworking, permaculture design.

Weismann, Adam, and Katy Bryce. 2006. *Building with Cob: A Step-by-Step Guide*. Totnes, Devon: Green Books.

Dry-stone walls
Burngate Stone Carving Centre. burngatestonecentre.co.uk. Offers courses in the United Kingdom in stone carving, sculpture, and more.

Dry Stone Conservancy. www.drystone.org. Aims to preserve historic dry-stone structures, to advance the dry-stone masonry craft, and to create a center for training and expertise.

Dry Stone Walling Association. www.dswa.org.uk. Promotes knowledge about the traditional craft of dry-stone walling and encourages the repair and maintenance of dry-stone walls throughout the country.

National Stone Centre. www.nationalstonecentre.org.uk. Offers courses and workshops in dry-stone wall construction.

Ty-Mawr Lime Ltd. www.lime.org.uk/courses. Offers courses in dry-stone walling and lime plastering.

6: BASIC PRINCIPLES OF SUSTAINABLE PLANTING DESIGN

Biodiversity in Urban Gardens in Sheffield. www.bugs.group.shef.ac.uk/BUGS1/bugs1-index.html. Research project focused on the significance of urban gardens for natural biodiversity.

Flora Locale. www.floralocale.org. U.K. organisation seeking to restore wild plants and wild plant communities to lands and landscapes.

Garden Organic Heritage Seed Library. www.gardenorganic.org.uk/hsl/. U.K. organisation working to safeguard rare vegetable varieties that were once the mainstay of British gardens.

International Society of Arboriculture. www.treesaregood.com. Website providing the general public with quality tree-care information.

Landlife. www.landlife.org.uk. U.K. organisation that works for a better environment by creating new opportunities for wildflowers and wildlife and encouraging people to enjoy them.

Lloyd, Christopher. 2004. *Meadows*. Portland, OR: Timber Press.

National Wildflower Centre. www.nwc.org.uk. U.K. organisation promoting new wildflower habitats through creative conservation.

Native Plant Information Network. www.wildflower.org/explore. Project of the Ladybird Johnson Wildflower Center at the University of Texas that assembles and disseminates information about the sustainable use of native wildflowers and plants throughout North America.

Nowak, David J., Daniel E. Crane, and John F. Dwyer. 2002. Carbon storage and sequestration by urban trees in the USA. *Environmental Pollution* 116: 381–89.

Royal Horticultural Society (RHS) Plant Finder. apps.rhs.org.uk/rhsplantfinder/index.asp. The place to search for suppliers of plants in the United Kingdom.

Seed Savers Exchange. www.seedsavers.org. U.S. organisation of gardeners dedicated to sharing and exchanging seeds.

Wild Ones. www.for-wild.org. U.S. organisation advocating native plants in natural landscapes.

7: PREPARING SOIL AND PLANTING

Canadian peat harvesting and the environment, 2nd edition. 2001. North American Wetlands Conservation Council Committee, Issues Paper No. 2001-1. www.peatmoss.com/pdf/Issuepap2.pdf

Canadian Sphagnum Peat Moss Association (CSPMA). www.peatmoss.com. Sets strict environmental guidelines for the harvesting of peat moss certified by the CSPMA seal.

Craul, Phillip J. 1992. *Urban Soil in Landscape Design*. New York: Wiley.

Dowding, Charles. 2007. *Organic Gardening: The Natural No-Dig Way*. Totnes, Devon: Green Books.

Eden Project. www.edenproject.com. Massive environmental centre in Cornwall that features the world's largest greenhouse and demonstrates the use of Strulch.

Elmer, Wade H. 2009. Influence of earthworm activity on soil microbes and soilborne diseases of vegetables. *Plant Disease* 93: 175-79.

Gilbert, Oliver L. 1989. *The Ecology of Urban Habitats*. London: Chapman and Hall.

Patterson, J. C., J. J. Murray, and J. R. Short. 1980. The impact of urban soils on vegetation. *Metropolitan Tree Improvement Alliance Proceedings* 3: 1–14.

Soil Association. www.soilassociation.org. U.K. nonprofit promoting planet-friendly food and farming.

8: SELECTING PLANTS FOR CHALLENGING CONDITIONS

Huxman, Travis E., Melinda D. Smith, Philip A. Fay, Alan K. Knapp, M. Rebecca Shaw, Michael E. Loik, Stanley D. Smith, David T. Tissue, John C. Zak, Jake F. Weltzin, et al. 2004. Convergence across biomes to a common rain-use efficiency. *Nature* 429: 651-54.

Powell, M. A. 1993. Conserving energy with plants. North Carolina Cooperative Extension Service leaflet #631. www.ces.ncsu.edu/depts/hort/hil/hil-631.html.

10: GARDENING WITH WILDLIFE IN MIND

American Beekeeping Federation. www.abfnet.org. U.S. organisation that works in the interests of beekeepers to ensure the future of the honeybee.

Baines, C. *How to Make a Wildlife Garden*. 1985. Elm Tree Books. Revised and reprinted as a paperback, 2000, London: Frances Lincoln.

British Beekeepers' Association. Bees4Kids—Importance of Bees. www.britishbee.org.uk/bees4kids/index.php.

Butterfly Conservation. www.butterfly-conservation.org. U.K. organisation working to promote butterfly species

Fountain, M. F., R. Day, C. Quartley, and A. Goatcher. 1991. *Garden Plants Valuable to Bees*. International Bee Research Association. ibrastore.org.uk/index.php?main_page=product_info&products_id=48.

Invertebrate Conservation Trust. www.buglife.org.uk. U.K. organisation devoted to the conservation of invertebrates.

Lewis, Pam. 2007. *Sticky Wicket: Gardening in Tune with Nature*. London: Frances Lincoln.

National Bee Supplies. www.beekeeping.co.uk. U.K. supplier of beekeeping equipment.

Royal Society for the Protection of Birds. www.rspb.org.uk. U.K. charity working to protect birds and the environment.

Vickery, Margaret. 1998. *Gardening for Butterflies*. Wareham, Dorset: British Butterfly Conservation Society.

Wildlife Trusts. www.wildlifetrusts.org. U.K. voluntary organisation dedicated to conserving habitats and species.

Xerces Society. www.xerces.org. Nonprofit organization that protects wildlife through the conservation of invertebrates and their habitat.

11: GROWING YOUR OWN FOOD AND CUT FLOWERS

Food

Ashworth, Suzanne. 2002. *Seed to Seed: Seed Saving and Growing Techniques for Vegetable Gardeners*. Decorah, IA: Seed Savers Exchange.

ELT EasyGreen Living Wall System. www.eltlivingwalls.com/living-walls/. In North America, ELT offers a living wall system built around modular planted panels.

Garden Organic. www.gardenorganic.org.uk. Leading U.K. organic growing charity offering advice, heritage seeds, and gardens to visit.

Guerra, Michael. 2005. *The Edible Container Garden: Fresh Food from Tiny Spaces*. London: Gaia Books.

Kitchen Gardeners International. www.kitchengardeners.org. Community of 20,000 kitchen gardeners from more than 100 countries who network through blogs and forums.

Sarah Raven's Garden and Cookery School. www.sarahraven.com/perch-hill. Online gardening shop of Sarah Raven, writer, cook, broadcaster, and teacher. Also offers cooking, flower arranging, growing, and gardening courses at her garden.

Trevakis Farm. www.trevaskisfarm.co.uk/education/. "A brand new education experience about the food we eat and where it is grown."

Valcent Products. www.valcent.net/s/HDVGS.asp. With offices in Canada, the United States, and the United Kingdom, Valcent offers VertiCrop, a high-density vertical growing system for commercial crops.

Veg Patch at River Cottage. www.rivercottage.net. Website of writer and broadcaster Hugh Fearnley-Whittingstall, with details about the River Cottage Foods business: "about food, where it comes from, and why that matters."

VertiGarden. www.vertigarden.co.uk/. Vertical gardening systems for the home gardener in the United Kingdom.

Walled Kitchen Gardens Network. www.walledgardens.net. Association celebrating walled kitchen gardens, aiming to support their renaissance.

Warren, Piers. 2008. *How to Store Your Garden Produce: The Key to Self-Sufficiency*, 2nd ed. Totnes, Devon: Green Books.

Flowers
Association of Local Cut Flower Growers. www.ascfg.org. Informs growers on the production and marketing of field and greenhouse cut flowers.

Beutler, Linda. 2007. *Garden to Vase: Growing and Using Your Own Cut Flowers*. Portland: Timber Press.

Catkin Flowers. www.catkinflowers.co.uk. Floristry service offering flowers grown in a sustainable way in order to reduce the environmental impact of the business.

Raven, Sarah. 2006. *The Cutting Garden: Growing and Arranging Garden Flowers*. London: Frances Lincoln.

VeriFlora. www.veriflora.com. Certifies sustainably grown potted plants and flowers in the United States and Canada. You can download a list of certified products and retailers from this website.

Walled Garden School. www.thewalledgardenatmells.co.uk/courses-at-the-walled-garden-school-mells.htm. U.K. garden school offering courses in how to grow, condition, and arrange flowers.

12: MAINTAINING THE GREENER GARDEN

Briggs, Michael. 2004. Widescale biodiesel production from algae. www.unh.edu/p2/biodiesel/article_alge.html.

Clean Air Lawn Care. www.cleanairlawncare.com. U.S. franchise business that offers sustainable lawn care.

Green Seal. 1998. Lawn care equipment. *Choose Green Report*, June/July. www.greenseal.org/resources/reports/CGR=LawnCareEquip.pdf.

Mutch, D., S. A. Thalmann, T. E. Martin, and D. G. Baas. 2008. Flaming as a method of weed control in organic farming systems. MSU Extension bulletin E-3038. www.mosesorganic.org/attachments/productioninfo/08flaming.pdf.

National Renewable Energy Laboratory. www.nrel.gov. U.S. federal laboratory dedicated to research, development, commercialization, and deployment of renewable energy and energy-efficiency technologies.

Reich, Lee. 2001. *Weedless Gardening*. New York: Workman.

U. S. Environmental Protection Agency. 1991. *Nonroad Engine and Vehicle Emission Study—Report*. Washington, DC: Office of Air and Radiation, U.S. Environmental Protection Agency. www.epa.gov/nonroad/nrstudy.pdf.

13: INCORPORATING ADVANCED FEATURES AND IDEAS

Agroforestry Research Trust. www.agroforestry.co.uk. Researches agroforestry, has developed a forest garden in Dartington, and publishes *Creating a Forest Garden* by Martin Crawford.

Bangor Forest Garden Project. www.thebfg.org.uk Forest garden set up by the University of Wales and run by students and volunteers.

Biodynamic Agricultural Association. www.biodynamic.org.uk. U.K. association offering biodynamic training courses and accreditation for the Demeter symbol.

Biodynamic Farming and Gardening Association. www.biodynamics.com. U.S. organisation for biodynamics research, development, and education.

Demeter USA. demeter-usa.org. Certifies biodynamic farms and products.

Dunnett, Nigel, and Andy Clayden. 2007. *Rain Gardens: Managing Water Sustainably in the Garden and Designed Landscape*. Portland, OR: Timber Press.

Dunnett, Nigel, and Noel Kingsbury. 2004. *Planting Green Roofs and Living Walls*. Portland, OR: Timber Press.

Fern, Ken. 2000. *Plants for a Future: Edible and Useful Plants for a Healthier World*. East Meon, Hampshire: Permanent Publications.

Leenhardt, Jacques, and Anna Lambertini. 2007. *Vertical Gardens*. Florence, Italy: Verba Volant.

Low Impact Development Center. www.lowimpactdevelopment.org/raingarden_design/templates.htm. U.S. organisation offering a selection of rain garden templates.

Naturewise. www.naturewise.org.uk. U.K. permaculture organisation that has planted a forest garden in Wales.

Permaculture Association. www.permaculture.org.uk. U.K. permaculture organisation supporting people to learn about permaculture.

Permaculture Institute. www.permaculture.org. U.S. organisation offering courses in permaculture and sustainable living.

Plants for a Future. www.pfaf.org/index.php. Resource centre for rare and unusual plants, particularly those with edible, medicinal, and other uses. Maintains separate U.K. and U.S. plant databases.

Reading International Solidarity Centre. www.risc.org.uk. U.K. organisation promoting action for sustainable development, human rights, and social justice. The forest roof garden on the building has open days posted on the website.

Regenerative Design Institute. www.regenerativedesign.org. U.S. nonprofit organisation offering courses in permaculture.

Whitefield, Patrick. 2002. *How to Make a Forest Garden*, 3rd edition. East Meon, Hampshire: Permanent Publications.

———. 2005. *The Earth Care Manual: A Permaculture Handbook for Britain and Other Temperate Countries*. East Meon, Hampshire: Permanent Publications.

ACKNOWLEDGEMENTS

This book would not have been possible without the incredible work and involvement of so many people. A big thank you to my editor, Lorraine Anderson, for her tactful suggestions, to my commissioning editor Anna Mumford, and to everyone else at Timber Press who worked on this project.

The material in this book is a result of long arguments, tips, research, and getting a few things terribly wrong. Thanks must go to the horticulturalists, growers, builders, writers, designers, and other industry experts who have been willing to share their knowledge with me. I should particularly mention Chris Marchant and the team at Orchard Dene Nurseries for allowing me to take photographs of their sumptuous perennials.

I couldn't have done any of this without the huge support behind the scenes from Jules, the unsung hero. Huge thanks also to the fantastic Daisy Holliday, who kept the office shipshape whilst I was distracted. You have been endlessly patient.

This book is dedicated to my grandparents, who ignited my passion for gardening many long years ago with a christening gift of life membership to the National Trust for Scotland. And to my mother, for her unwavering support, and for lending me her garden to play with when I didn't have a space of my own. Thank you.

INDEX

Photo by JOMO

ABOUT THE AUTHOR

Alice Bowe's work aims to demonstrate that you don't have to compromise on design in order to create and maintain a greener garden. An artist, garden designer, and author who draws inspiration from all aspects of art, architecture, and design, Alice is passionate about gardens and firmly believes in working with nature, not against it. Her fresh approach to sustainable garden design delivers stylish gardens that use resources efficiently—saving time, money, effort, and materials.

A well-known writer on hardworking garden design and planting, Alice regularly contributes to *The Times* of London and more occasional pieces for other magazines and newpapers, including *Gardens Illustrated* and *The Garden Design Journal*. Alice also appears on television and has been on the BBC presenting team for the RHS Chelsea Flower Show.

Alice inherited her green fingers from her grandparents, a talent she later combined with a passion for colour. She studied Fine Art at Oxford University, where she has since given lectures on planting design, and was elected a Fellow of the Royal Society of Arts in 2009.